Oatland Island

PHOTOGRAPHS AND HISTORY

Tara Jan Parekh

Published by Tara Jan Parekh

ISBN 978-0-6151-4909-7

Photography, Text, and Book Design by Tara Jan Parekh.

Forward

I began my exploration of Oatland Island in January, 2007. I was a graduate student at the Savannah College of Art and Design pursuing a Master of Arts degree in Digital Photography. I ventured over to Oatland Island one Saturday morning in search of a project for one of my classes. After walking the trails and observing the animals, I returned to meet the staff and discuss my project. Initially, I was interested in documenting the animals and the educational aspects of the center, but little did I know that I would become more intrigued by the history of the building and my discoveries within it.

This book showcases the images I have taken inside the Oatland Island facilities, the history of Oatland Island, and other stories I discovered along the way.

Oatland Island Wildlife Center is located five miles east of Savannah, Georgia. If you have never been, it is definitely worth a visit.

Acknowledgements

I owe special thanks to the staff members of Oatland Island Wildlife Center and to the Friends of Oatland Island. During the time I spent working on this project you made me feel like a part of Oatland Island Wildlife Center. Thank you for all of your help and encouragement.

Thank you to Dr. James W. Miles for educating me on the history of Oatland Island. It was a pleasure meeting you, listening to your stories, and learning about your scientific background.

Thank you to my friend Mary Wise for all of your editing help and guidance.

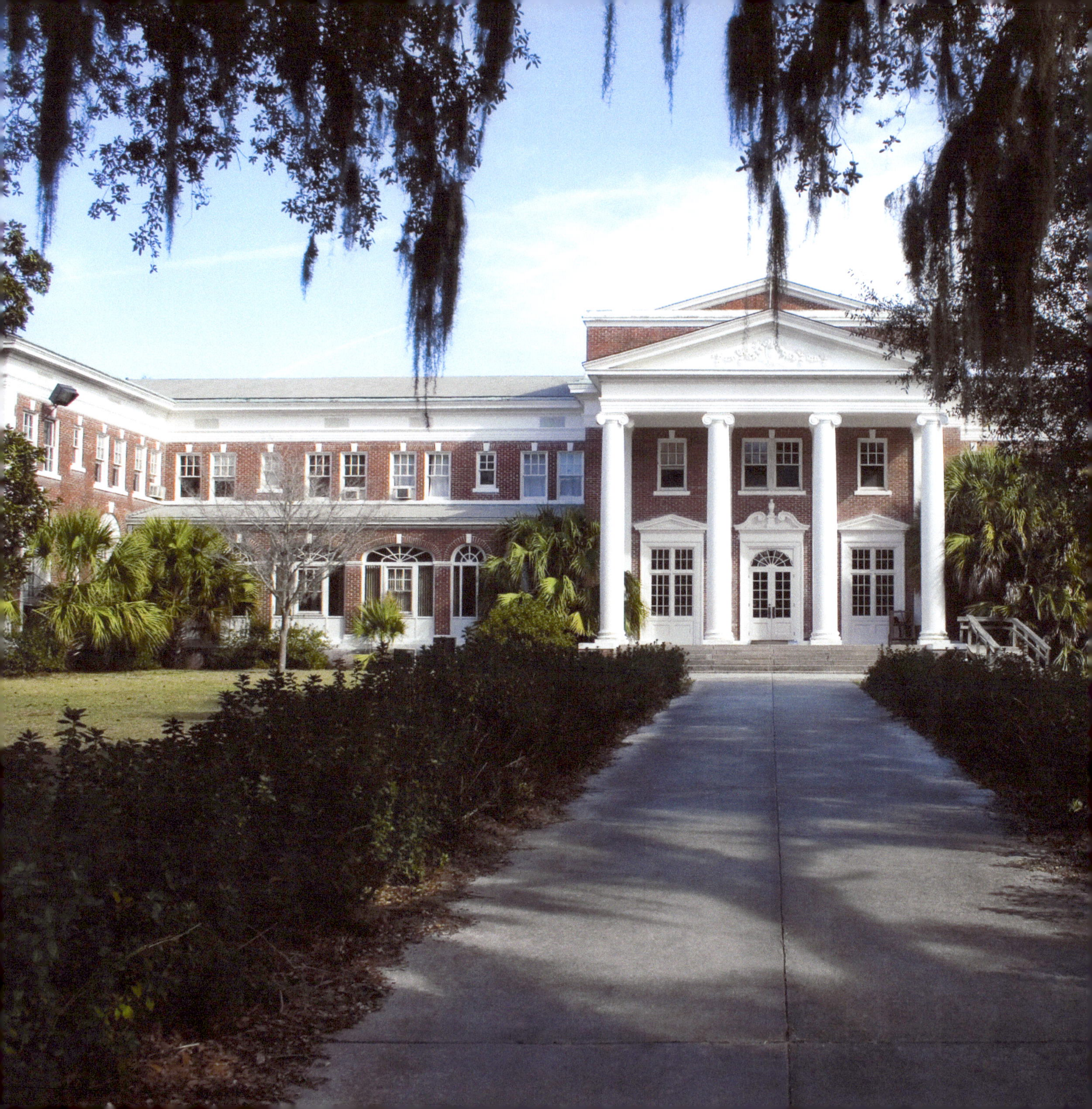

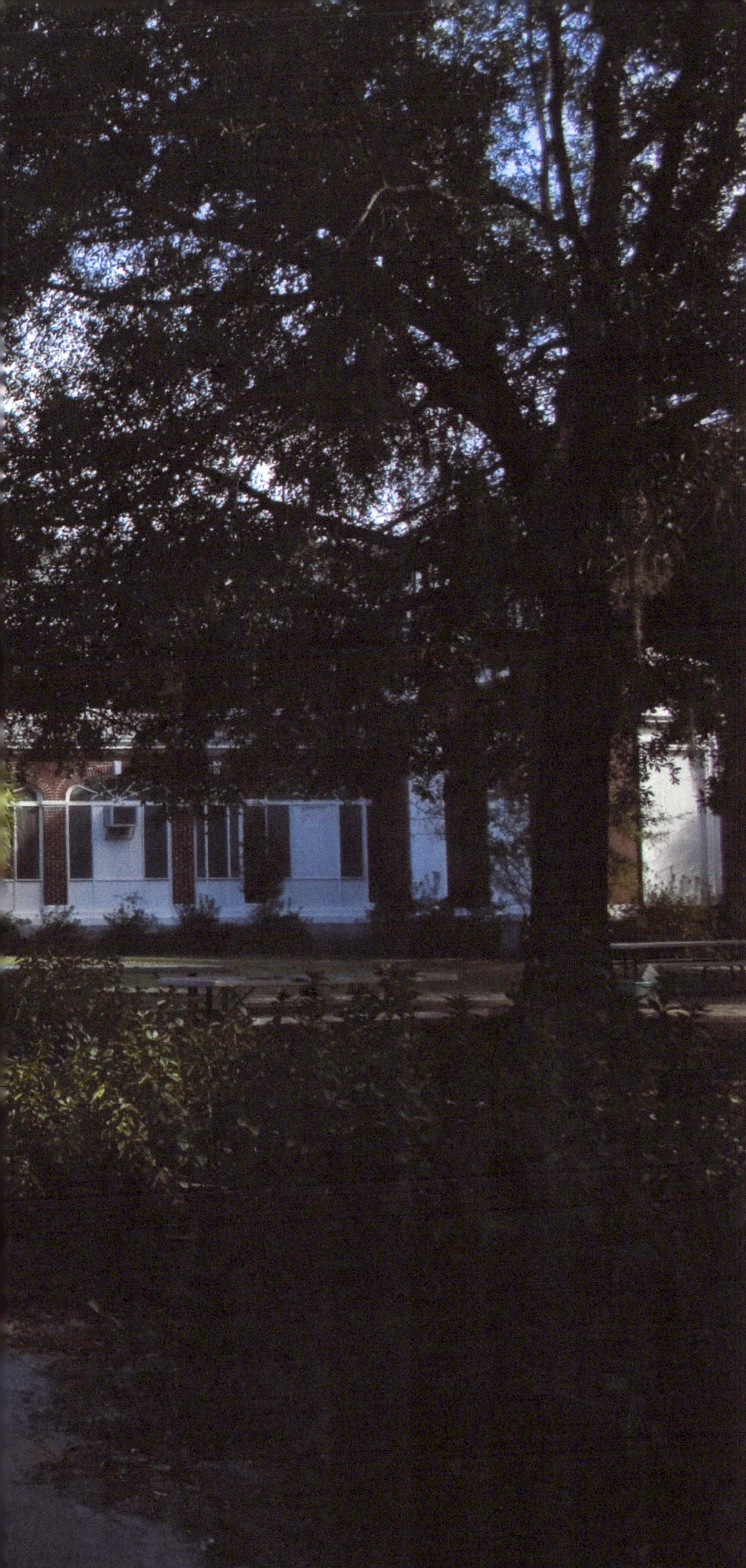

The History of Oatland Island

Perhaps the most fascinating part of exploring a place is discovering its history. When stepping onto the beautiful grounds of Oatland Island and looking upwards at the magnificent white ionic columns of the main building, it is natural to feel curious. Why was this building constructed? What was its purpose? As you will find out, the building on Oatland Island has had quite an interesting life. Although it is an education center today, the walls once housed railroad conductors, patients, scientists, inventors, and teachers.

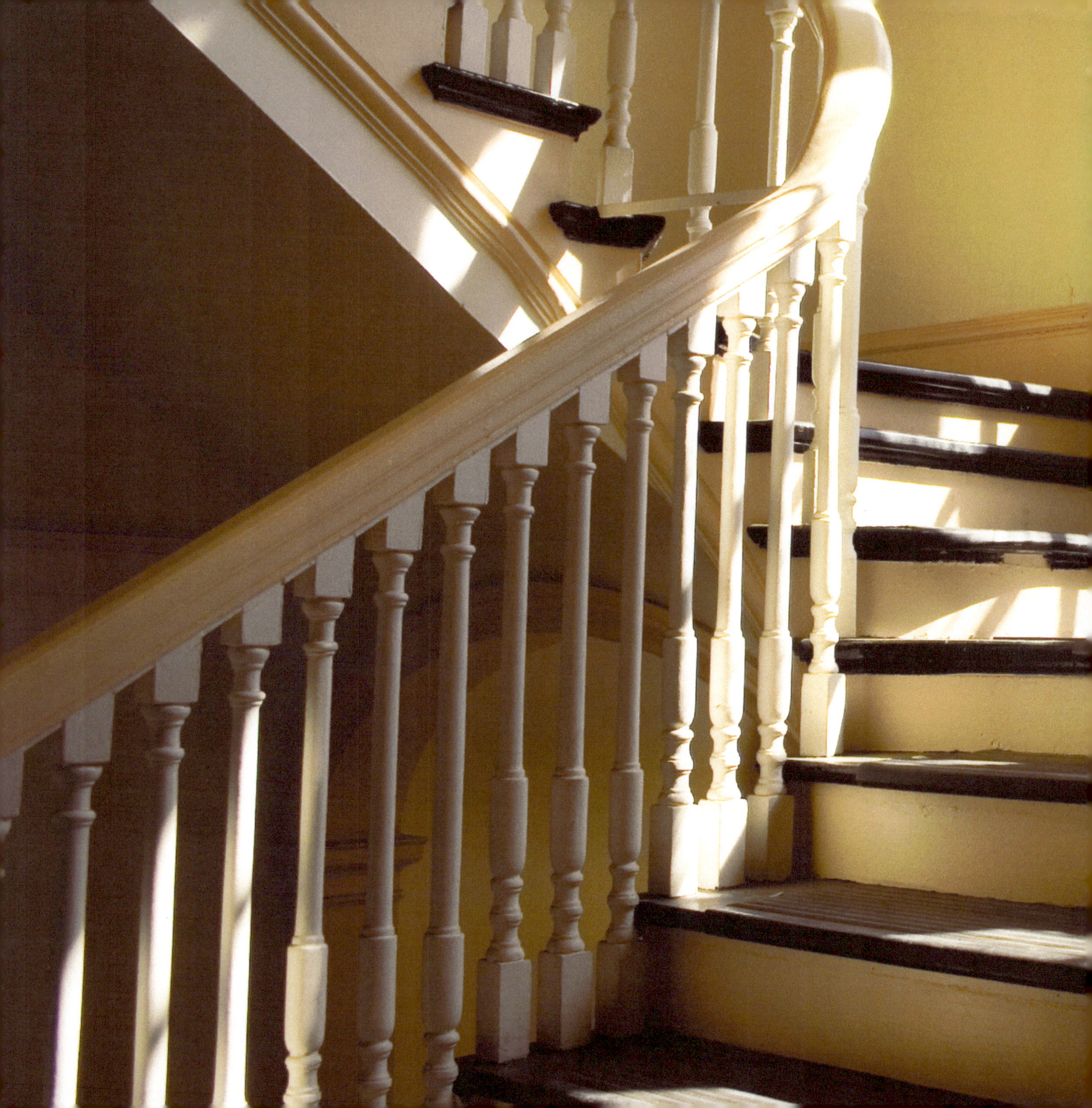

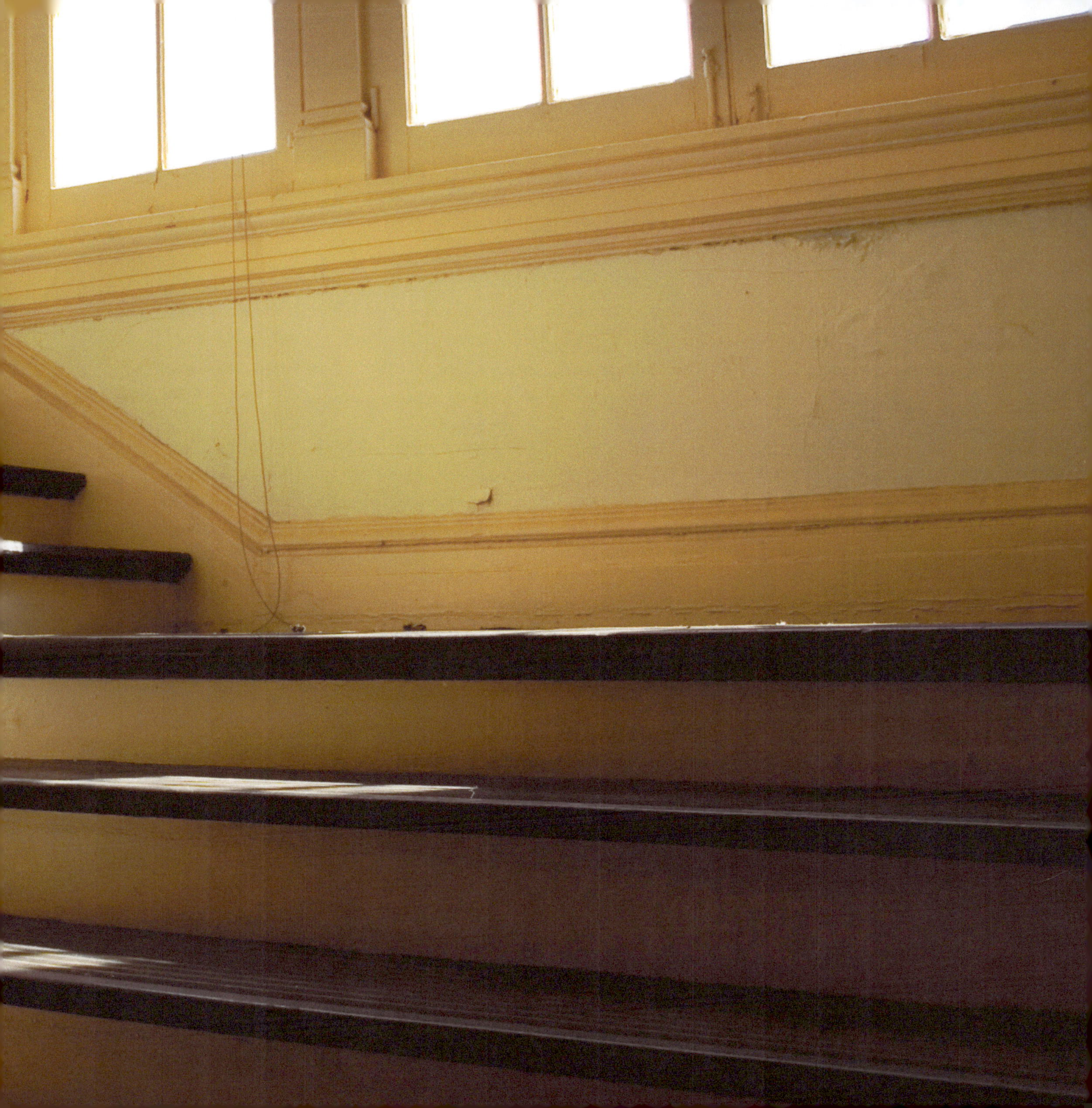

1927–1940

The Conductors Home: A Retirement Community for the Order of Railway Conductors

On November 12, 1927 after a brief ceremony, the building designed by the Savannah architects Wallin and Comer opened. The construction of the Conductors Home, a retirement community for the Order of Railway Conductors (ORC), began in April that year and cost a total of $350,000.00. H.C. Munn, a former railway conductor, had the idea of Savannah, Georgia being the site for the retirement home. After speaking with Mayor Hull, Munn acquired the Oatland site and construction began.

The building is constructed of brick, concrete, and cement. It is 240 feet long, has two wings, and faces westward towards Richardson Creek. It was considered to be nearly fire–proof because the only wooden constructions were the doors and the trimmings. The Conductors Home once contained 67 bedrooms, 21 on the main floor and the rest on the second floor. Six of the bedrooms had private baths, while the others had adjoining baths. Each room was furnished with a bed, a telephone, a telephone table, a dresser, a chair, a steam radiator, and a rug.

Entrance into the building was through the ivory–painted main lobby. There were brass lighting fixtures attached to the beamed ceiling, and a large staircase painted white and walnut led to the second floor. Walking through the first floor residents passed through French doors. The copper–screened windows were hung with beautiful draperies.

The north wing of the first floor contained a 400 square foot dining room and the kitchen. The kitchen was very modern because it featured electrically equipped coffee urns, a toaster, a washing machine, and an ice box. The south wing contained a lounge with wooden panel walls and a fireplace that was surrounded by stones from each state. The first floor also contained a glass–enclosed sun porch, the director's room, and a billiard room. The retirees even had hospitalization facilities located in one of the wings on the second floor.

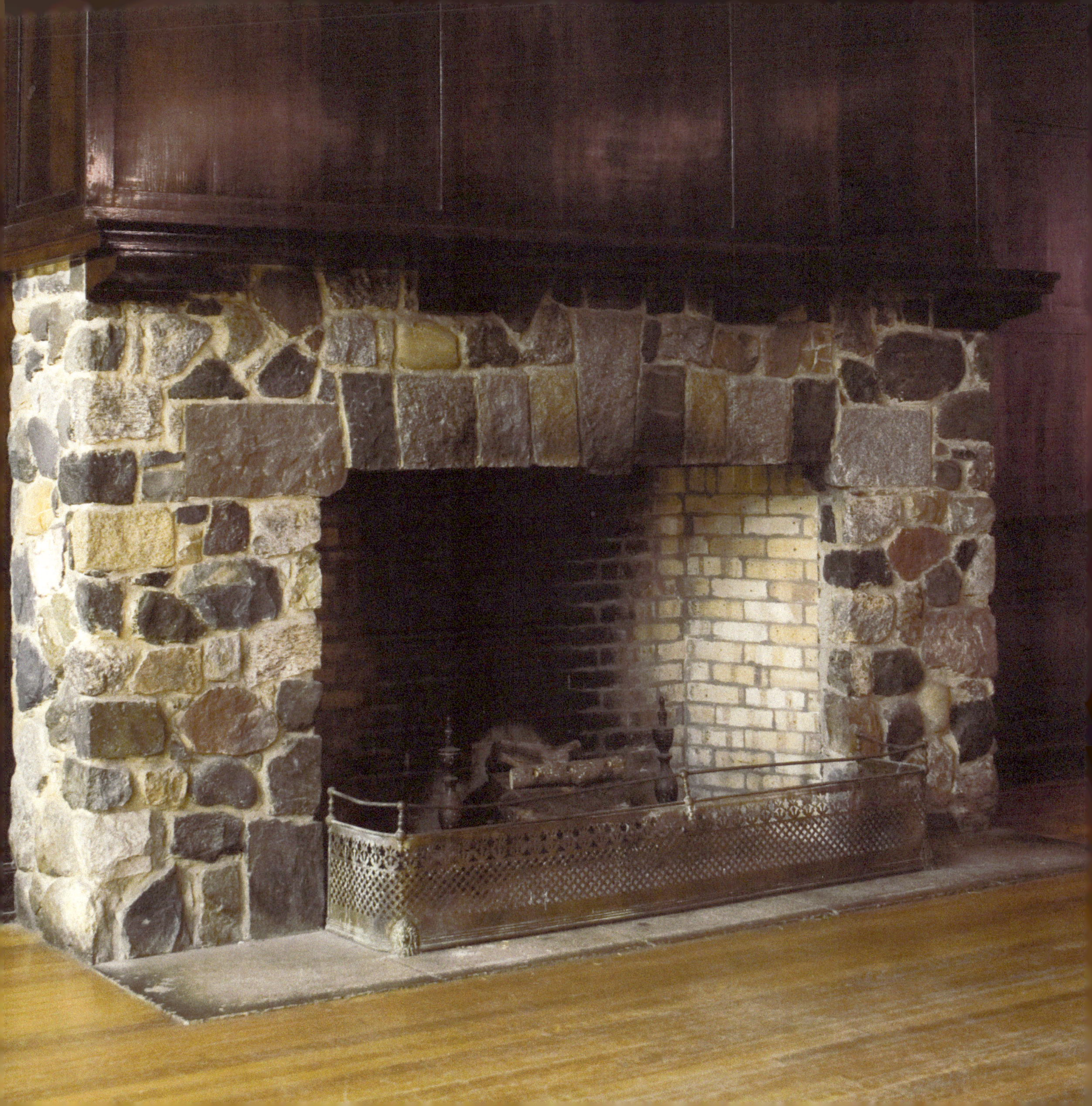

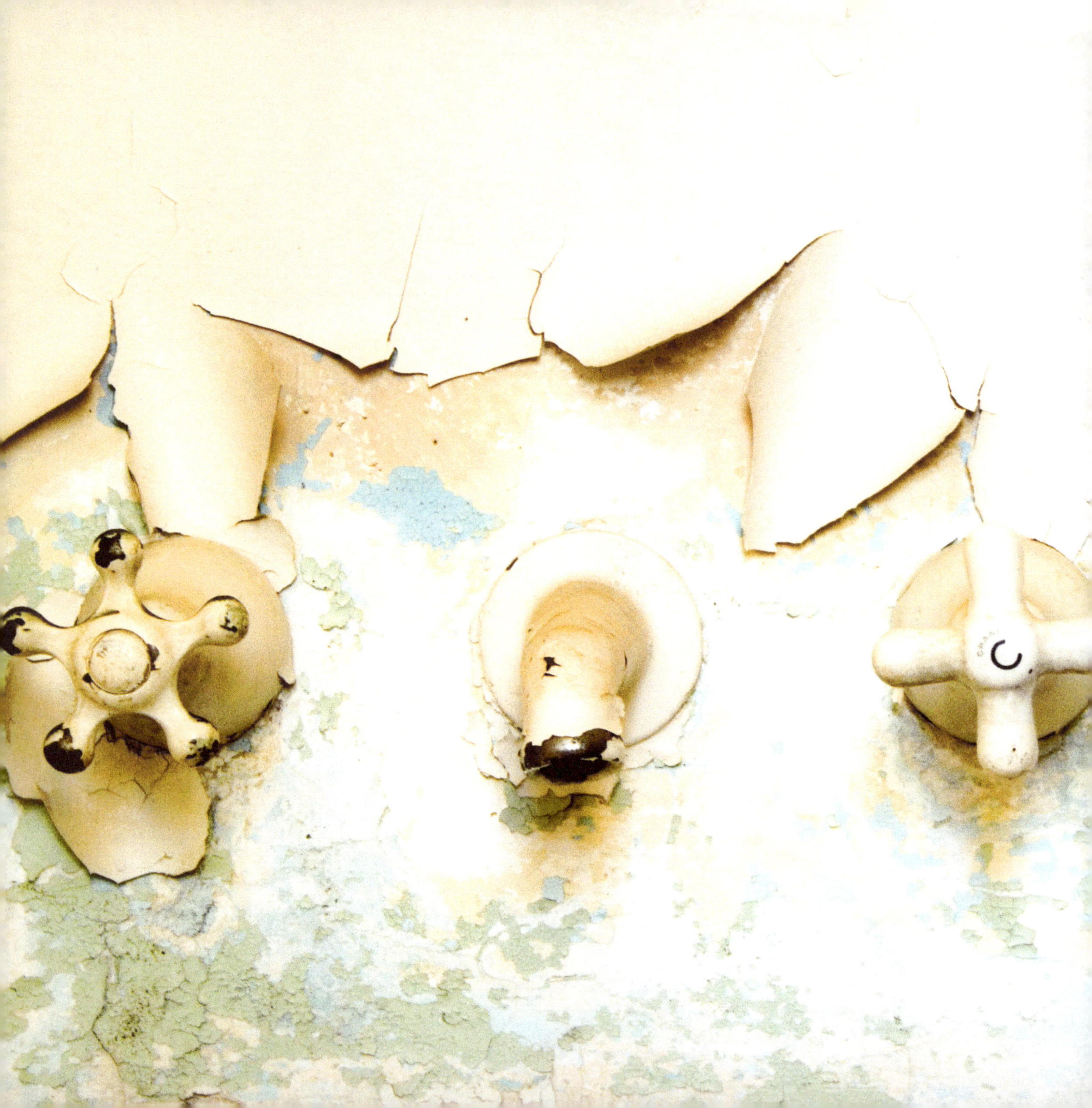

The retirement community was open to conductors, their wives, and widows of former conductors. When it opened in November of 1927, 14 members of the Order of Railway Conductors from Hylan Park, Illinois moved in. The members had served the Order for at least a quarter of a century, and most were disabled while on the job. The Conductors Home continued to flourish, but in 1940 the occupancy dropped down to only eleven retirees and their spouses, so the facility was closed.

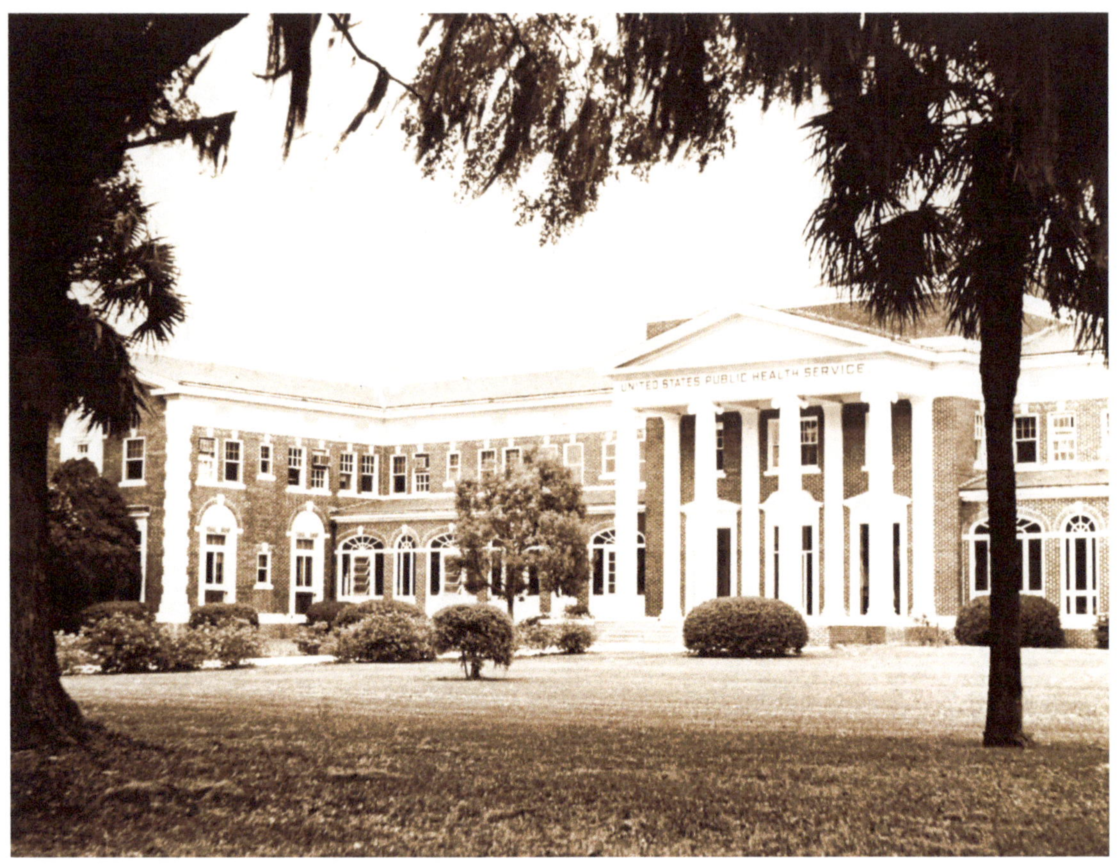

1941 – 1945

U.S. Public Health Service

In 1941, the Conductors Home was sold to the United States Public Health Service. The building was converted into a research hospital for woman and children that suffered from syphilis and other sexually transmitted diseases. The first floor contained doctor offices and the second floor housed the patients. There were numerous patients at Oatland at the time, and most stayed on bunk beds in the rooms.

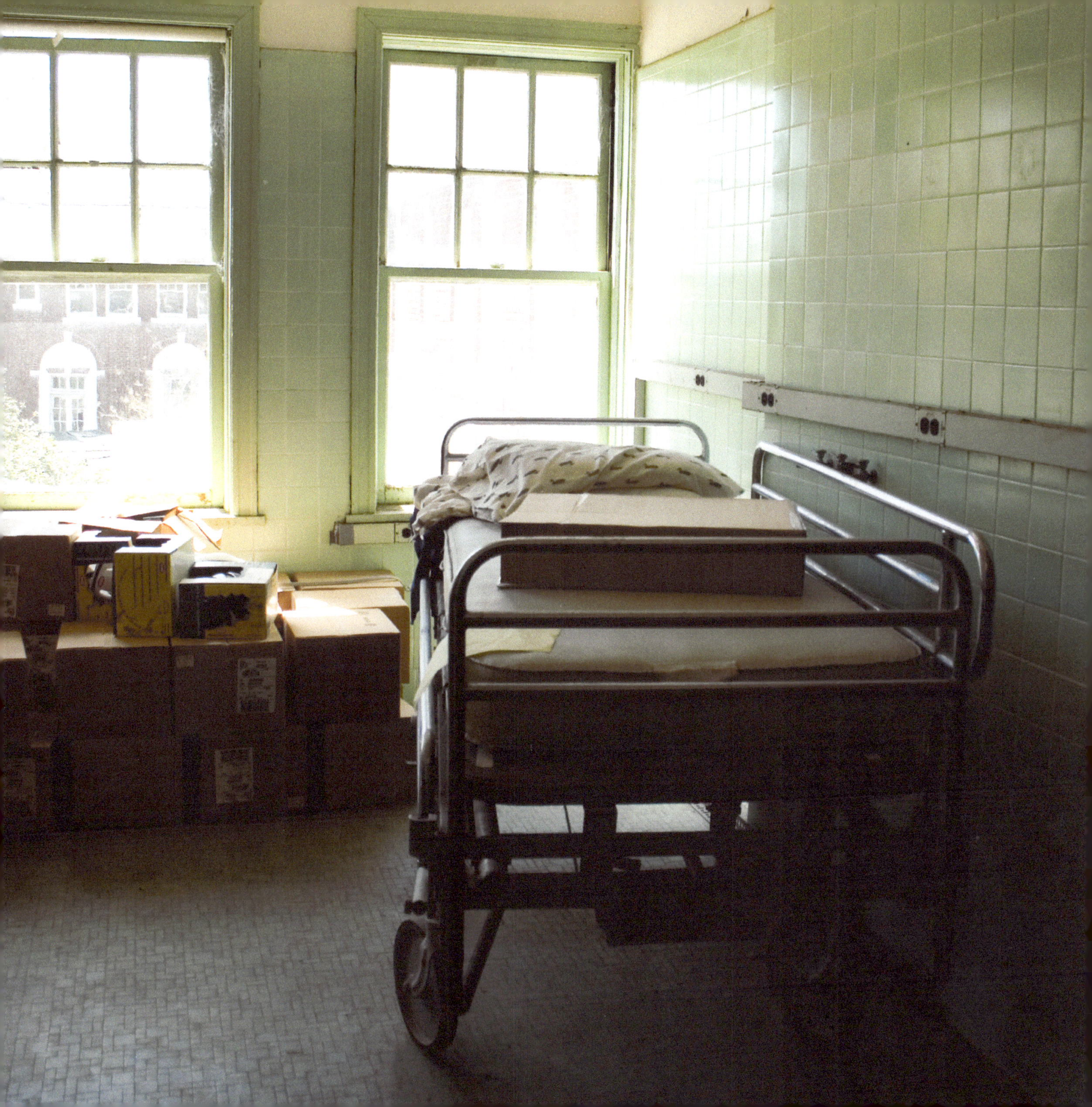

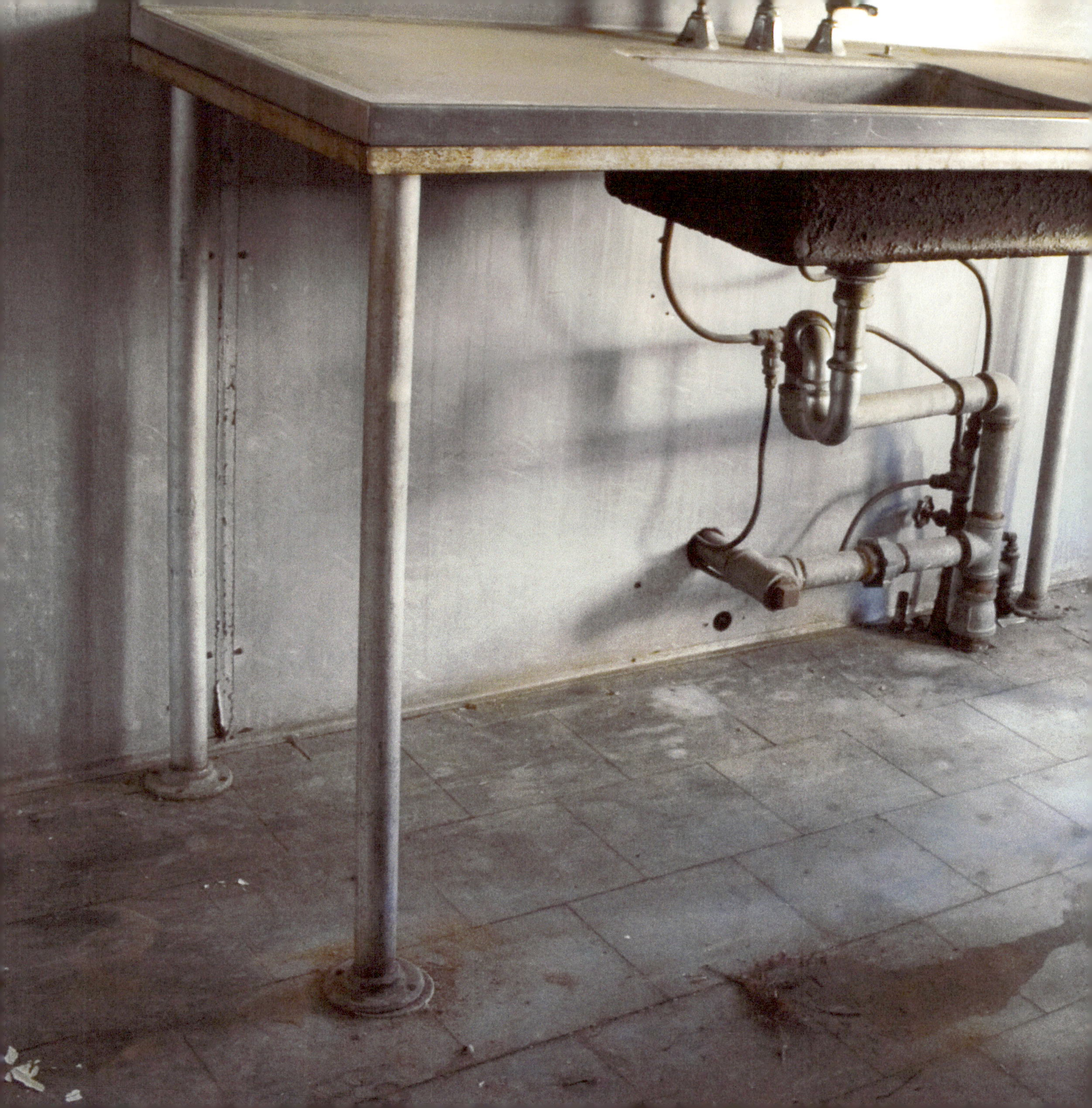

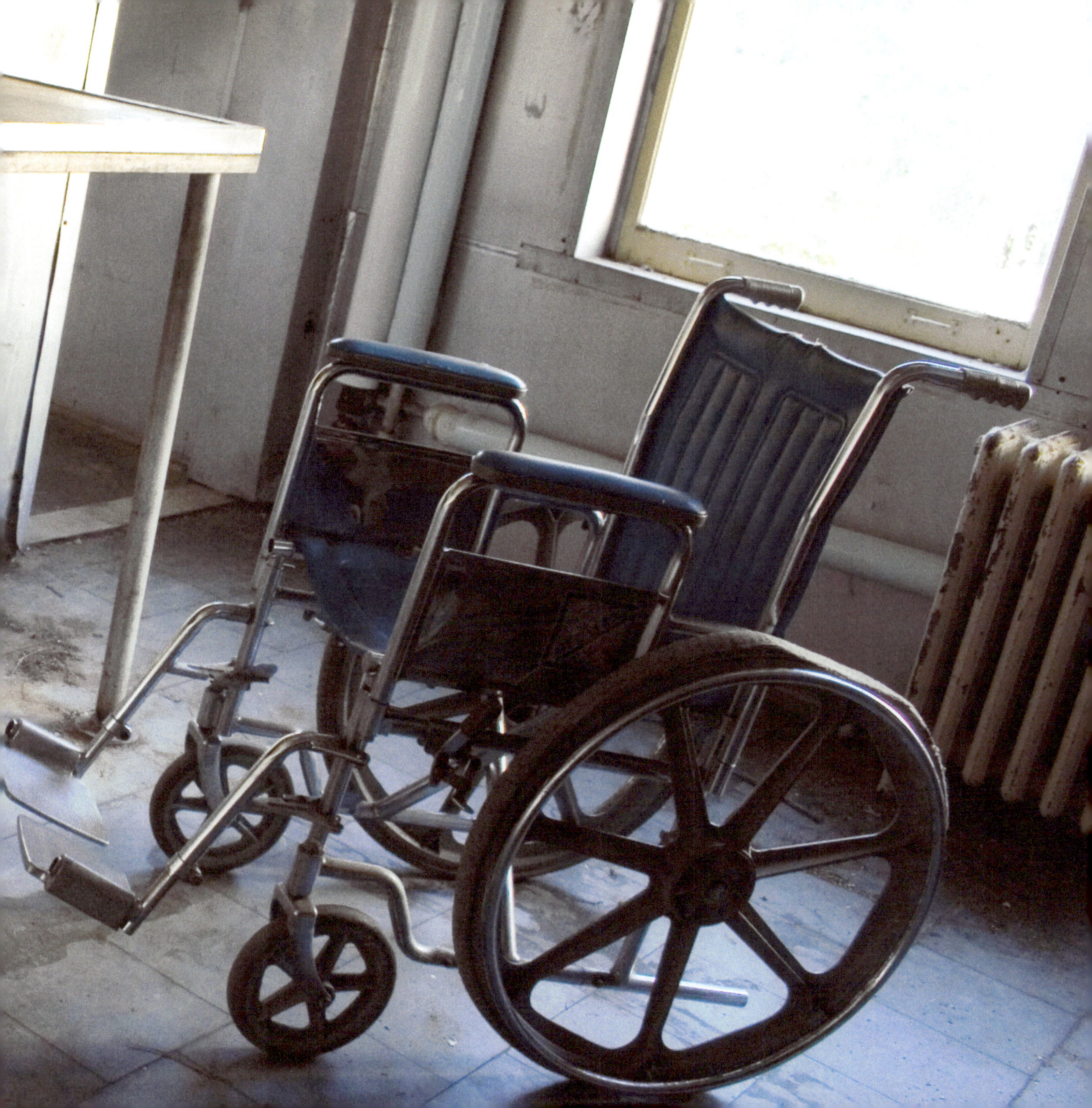

58
Blappity Bip
Heroin
MDA

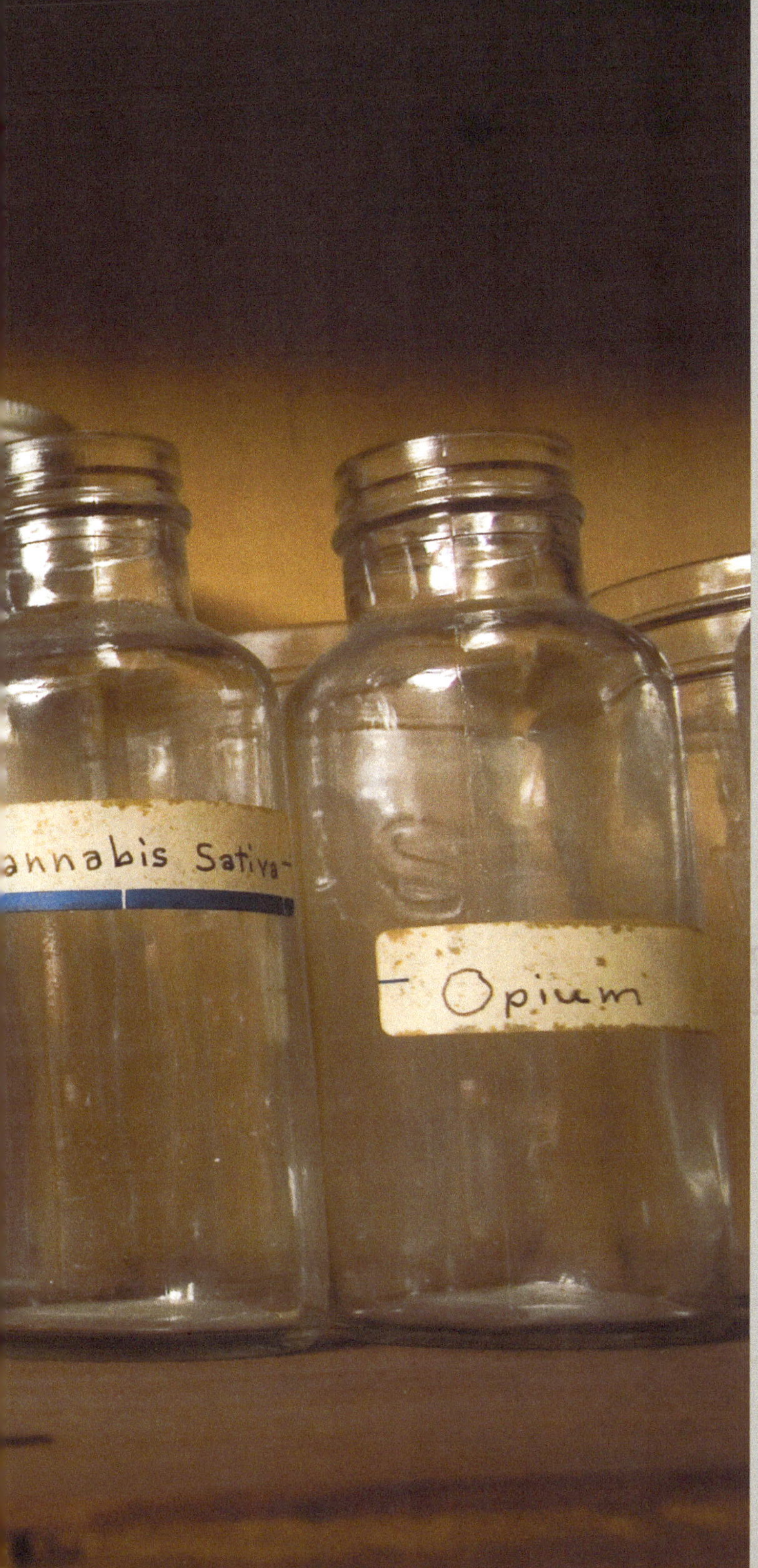

Many of the patients, including children, were in the late stages of the disease and had suffered from damage to their bones, teeth, eyes, ears, and brains. When penicillin, administered as a shot, became the cure for syphilis and other sexually transmitted diseases, the occupancy of the hospital decreased. It was closed in 1945. Although syphilis was no longer the threat it once had been, other diseases were still flourishing. Malaria, in particular, was a threat to the United States military.

1942

Malaria Control in War Areas:

Malaria Control in War Areas (MCWA) was established in 1942 in Atlanta, Georgia under the direction of Dr. Louis L. Williams Jr. Dr. Williams was an expert malariologist. Because of his military background he was aware of the threats malaria posed to the U.S. soldiers during World War II. The organization, a division of the United States Public Health Service, set out to limit malaria and vector–borne diseases around military training bases in the southern United States. At that time, MCWA was running operations out of Atlanta, and had recruited parasitologists, medical doctors, engineers, and entomologists. The problem was that MCWA lacked a research facility.

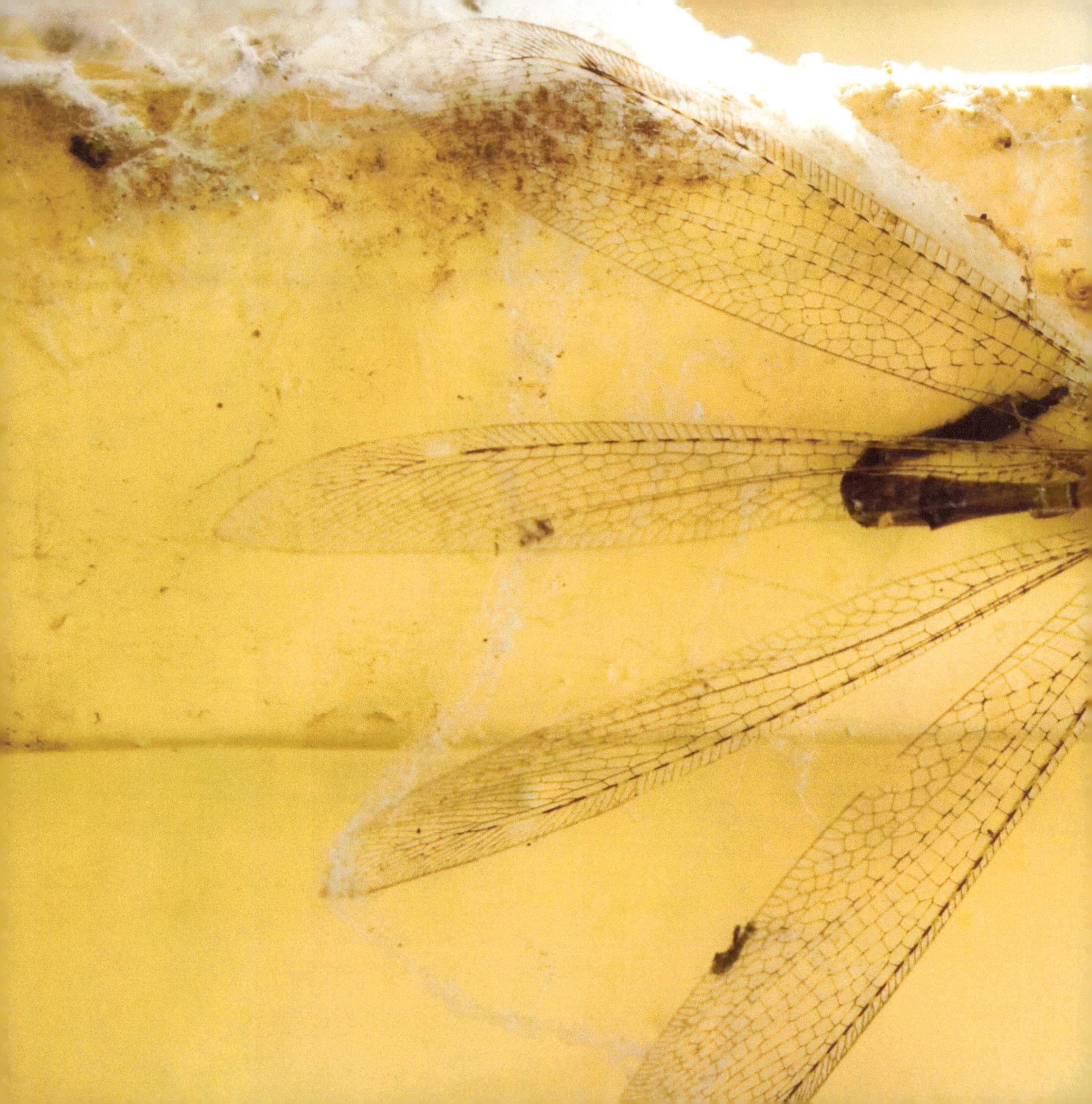

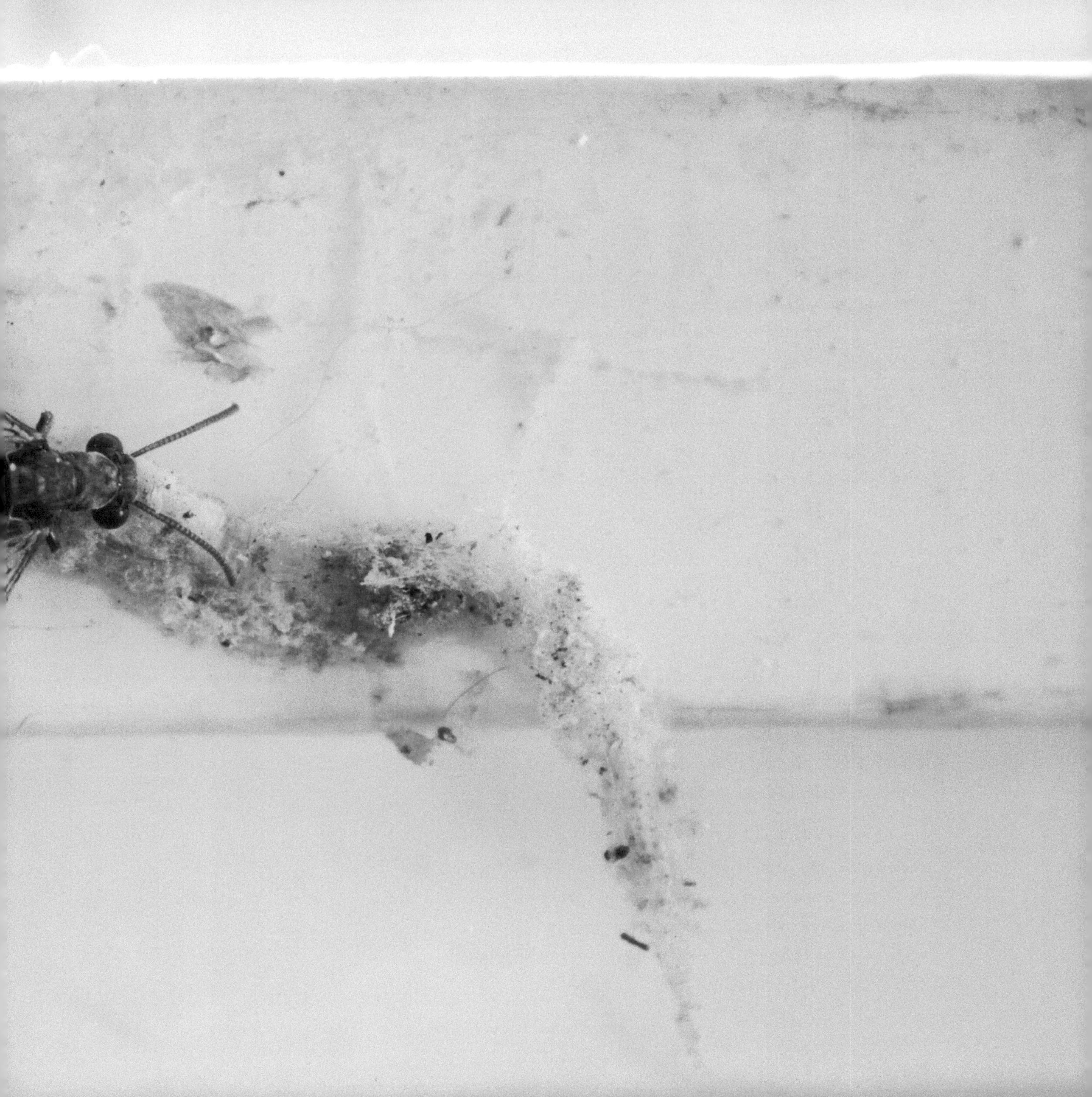

April 1944

Carter Memorial Laboratory

Luckily, Malaria Control in War Areas found a small research facility in Savannah, GA, known as the Carter Memorial Laboratory. The lab was already researching ways to control mosquitoes, and was eager to gain funding from the U.S. Public Health Service. In April of 1944, MCWA acquired the Carter Memorial Laboratory. Dr. Samuel W. Simmons directed its five staff members. As the staff grew, MCWA began looking for a larger facility. It was around that time when the U.S. Public Health Service hospital on Oatland Island closed, and the property was offered to MCWA. Dr. Simmons and his staff–now numbering 35–moved into the facility in July, 1946. At this time, MCWA changed its name to the Communicable Disease Center (CDC), known today as the Centers for Disease Control. In addition to malaria research, the CDC expanded its responsibilities for research on other diseases.

July 1946

Technical Development Laboratory (TDL)

After the move to Oatland Island, the Carter Laboratory was renamed the Technical Development Laboratory of the Communicable Disease Center. The Technical Development Laboratory was one of the world's leading laboratories that focused on mosquito biology, pesticide use and toxicology, and malaria control. From 1946 until 1973, the laboratory employed approximately 150 scientists, including members of the World Health Organization's expert committees.

Most of the research at the Technical Development Laboratory dealt with DDT, dichloro-diphenyltrichloroethane, and other synthetic organic pesticides. Othmer Zeidler, a German chemistry student, first discovered DDT in 1874. By combining chloral, a rapid-action sleeping potion, and chlorobenzene in sulfuric acid, Zeidler created a white precipitate of DDT crystals. At the time no one knew of its insecticidal properties. It wasn't until 1939 when Paul Müller, working for the Swiss Company, Geigy,

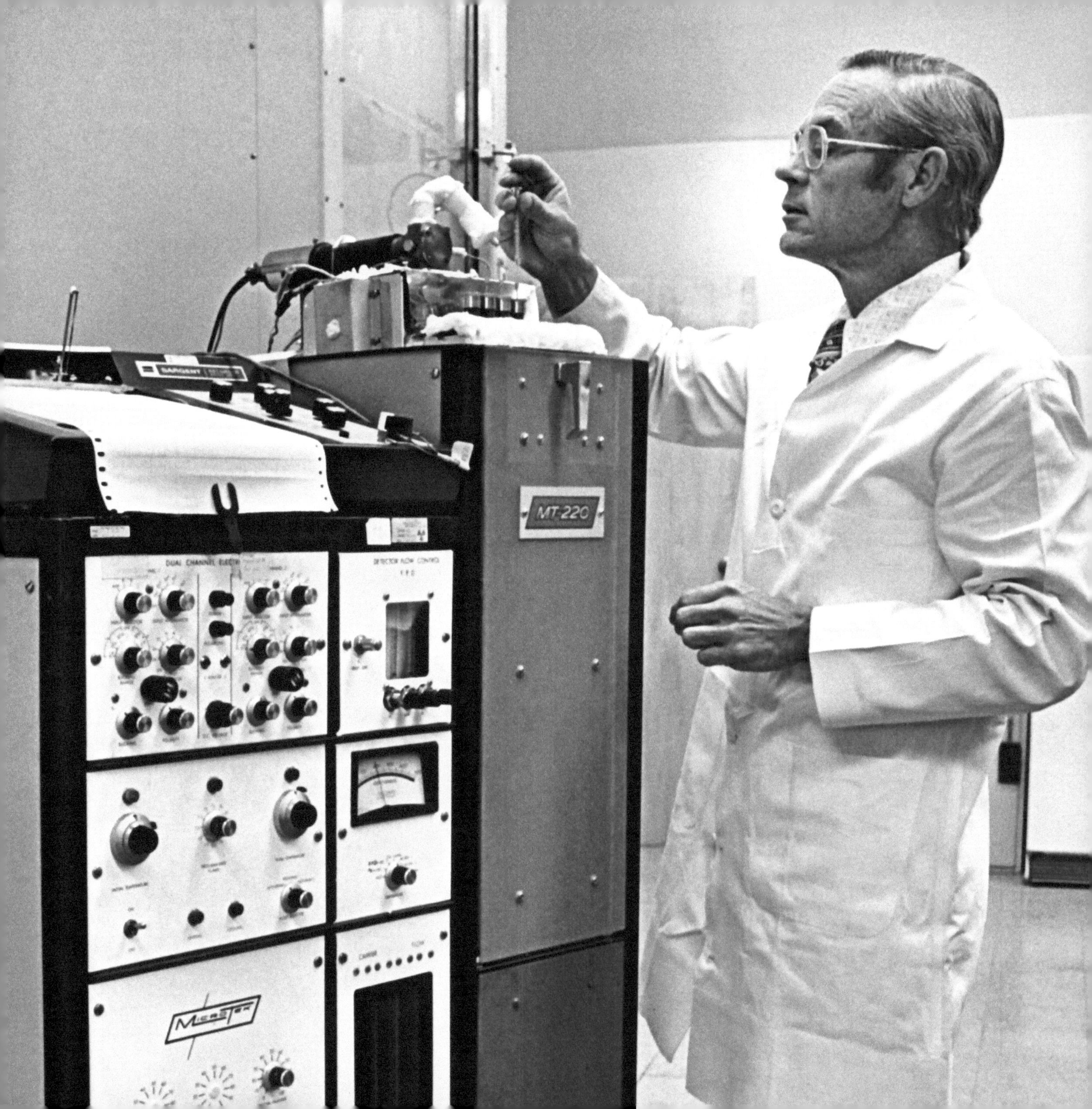
SARGENT
MT-220
DETECTOR FLOW CONTROL

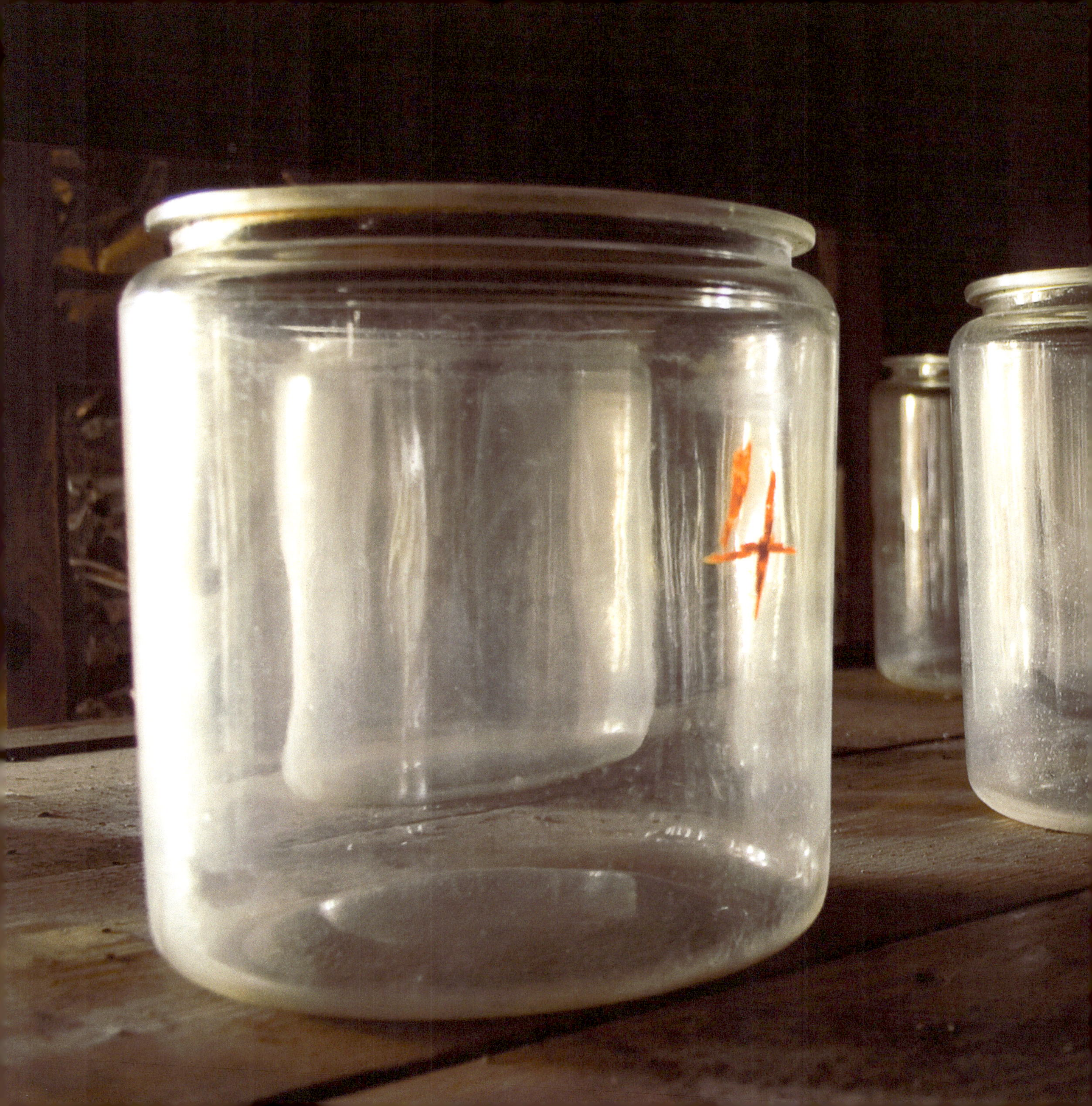
4

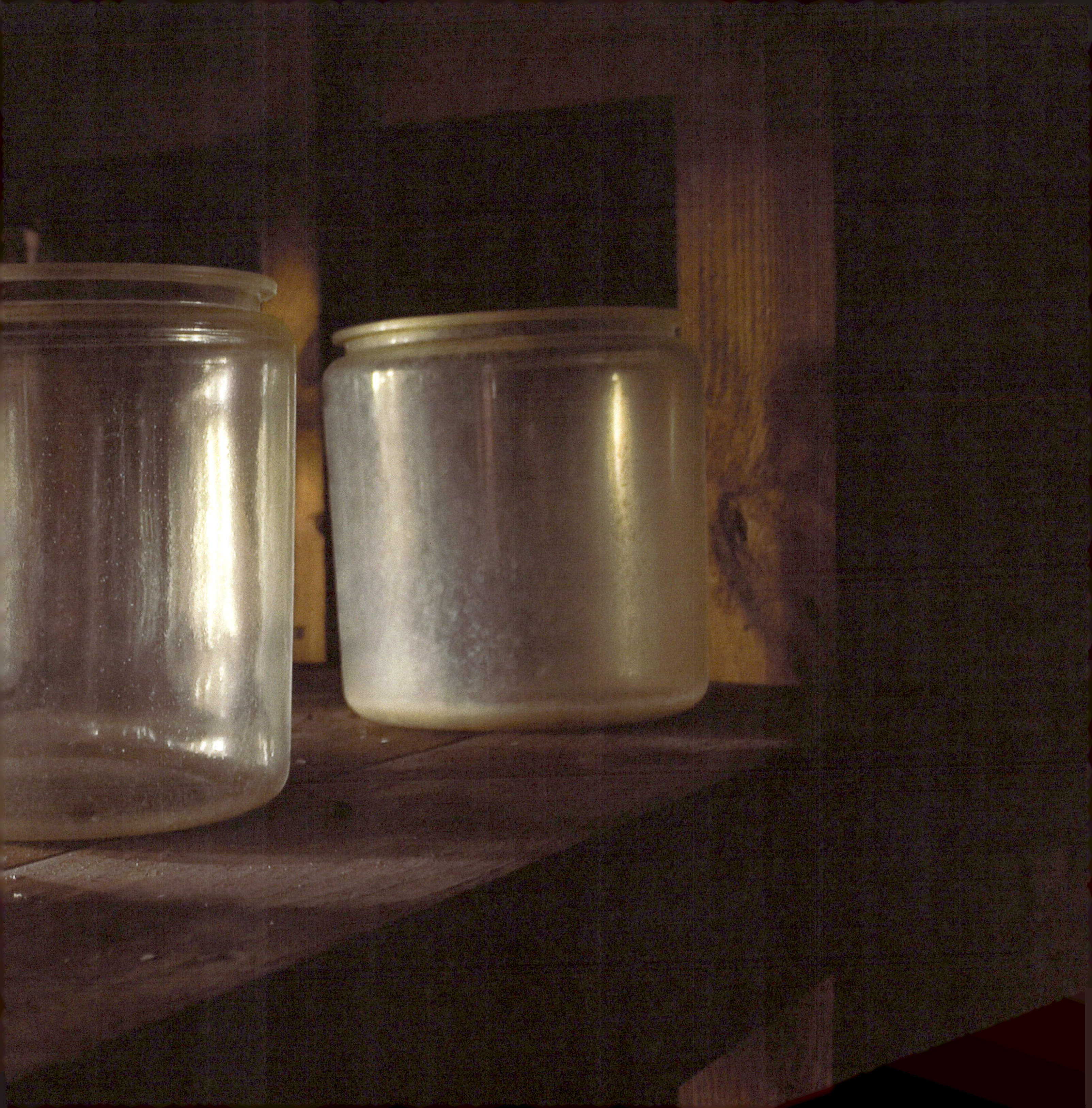

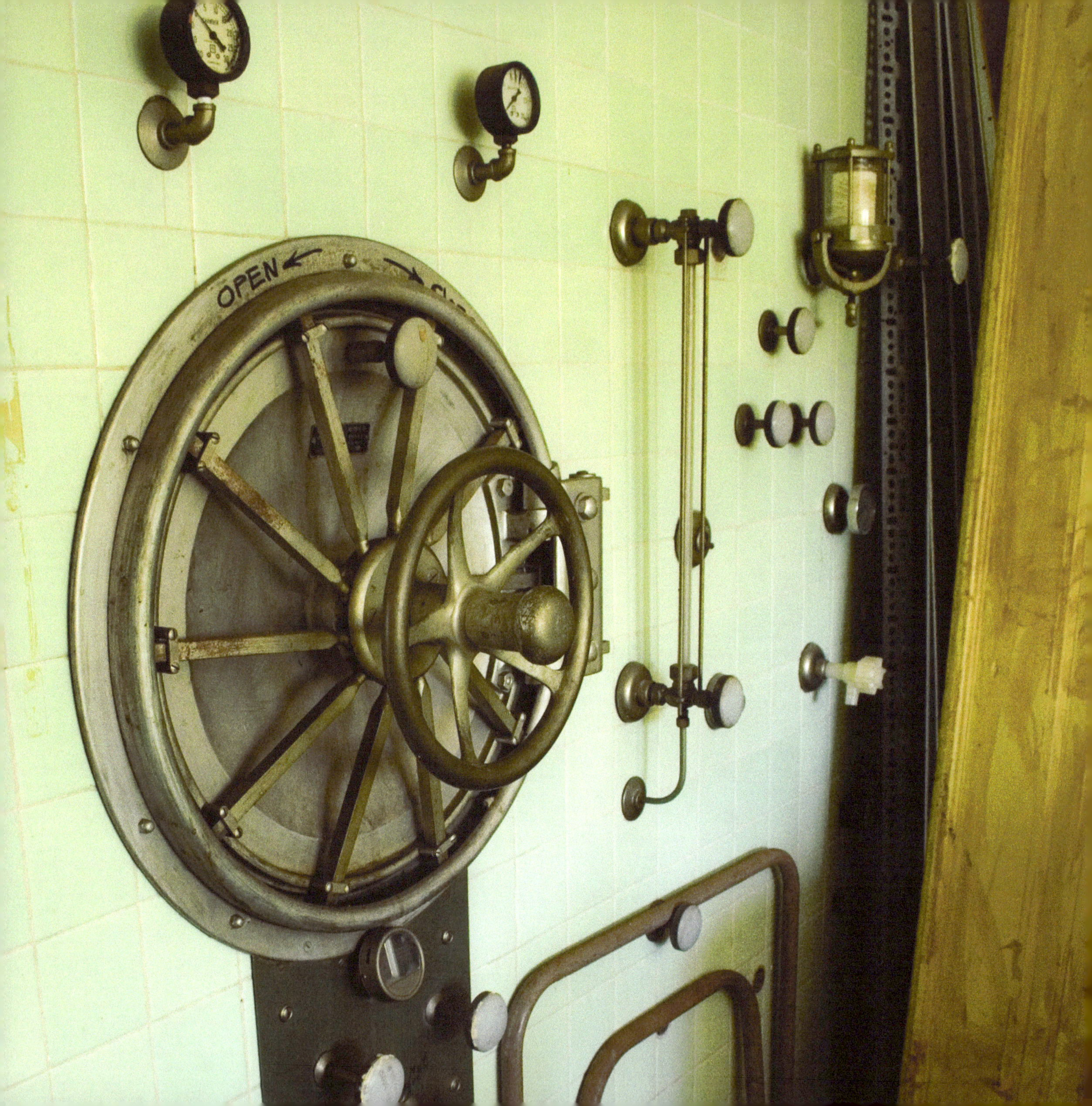
OPEN

tested DDT and discovered that it was an effective insecticide. Once it was proven effective against mosquitos carrying malaria, DDT was used for malaria control at the end of WWII. Soldiers sprayed themselves with low concentrations of DDT to control insects and mites.

Although DDT was cheap to manufacture and had low toxicity to mammals, entomologist feared that it might eliminate useful insects in addition to harmful insects. Samples of DDT powder were given to public health and agricultural laboratories including the Technical Development Laboratory. At the time, DDT was considered one of the safest compounds in use, but after nearly three decades since its application, the Environmental Protection Agency banned DDT on June 14, 1972.

1946–1973

Research at the Technical Development Laboratory

From 1946 until 1973, the Technical Development Laboratory conducted a variety of research that included studies on the insecticide DDT and its effect on humans, the discovery of the insecticide DDVP (Dichlorodimethyl vinyl phosphate or Dichlorvos), the use of radioisotopes, and procedural research on the disinsection of airplanes. The laboratory was considered to be an International Reference Center for the World Health Organization (WHO), and several staff members (Dr. Simmons, Dr. Ken Quarterman, Dr. George Pearce, Dr. Richard Fay, Dr. Herbert Schoof, and Dr. James Miles) were on the Advisory Panel of the WHO's Expert Committee on Vector Biology and Control.

The Sections of the Laboratory

Dr. Simmons organized the laboratory into four sections: Biology, Chemistry, Toxicology, and Biophysics. The Biology section occupied most of the second floor of the building and also was located in the greenhouse. The first floor and part of the annex contained the Chemistry section. In addition Dr. Hayes kept many animal cages throughout Oatland. The animals were used for experiments dealing with

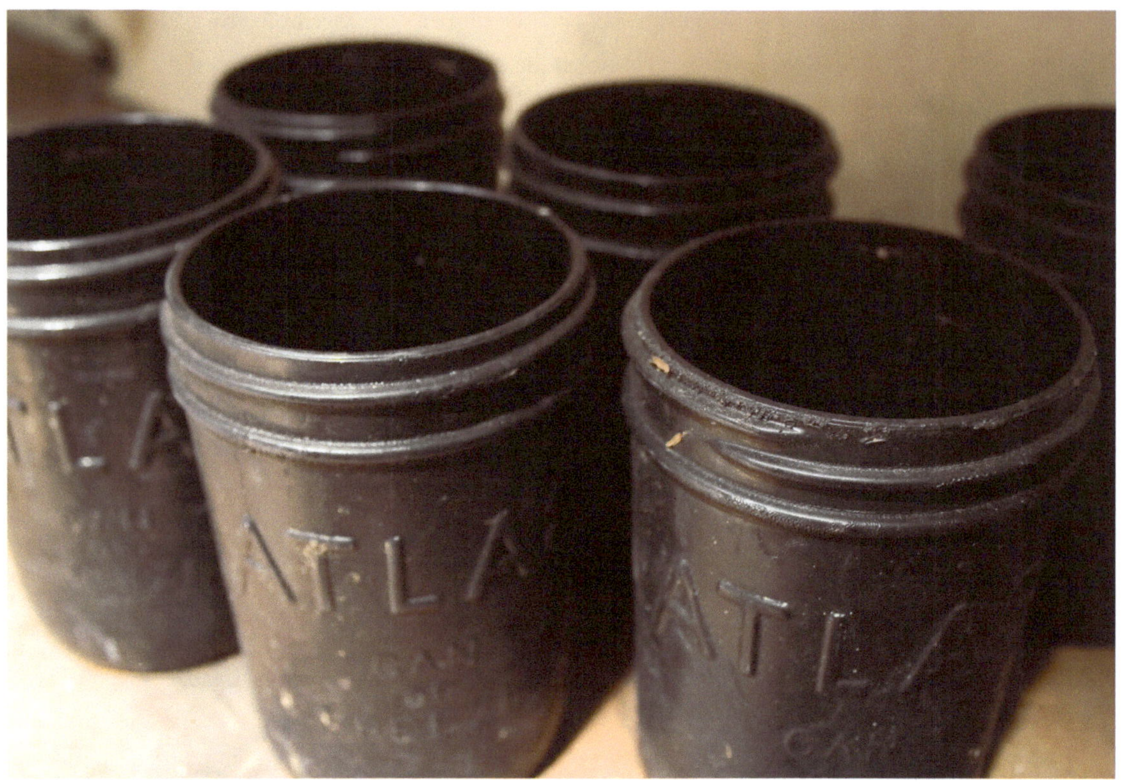

exposure to various pesticides. The Biophysics section was located in the metal buildings along the road just opposite the old water tower. Toxicology was located in the main building.

The Ovitrap, a Practical Invention

Dr. R.W. Fay, chief of the Biological Research unit, invented what he called an ovitrap while working at Oatland Island. By observing the mosquito in its natural habitat, Fay was able to learn that the females prefer to lay their eggs in dark, hidden places. His simple invention consisted of black-painted jar with a rough-surfaced paddle. The female mosquito would lay her eggs on this paddle, making egg collection easy.

Experimentation with Radioisotopes

Definition: A radioisotope is a radioactive isotope, a version of a chemical element that has an unstable nucleus and emits radiation during its decay to a stable form.

One experiment at Oatland Island was to use Phosphorus-32 to determine the flight range of mosquitoes. Mosquitoes in larval stages were immersed in a solution of sodium phosphate containing the radioisotope Phosphorus-32. Traps were set up at a variety of distances away from Savannah, Georgia. After 24 hours, the traps were collected and the mosquitoes were examined for radioactivity.

Mr. Jens A. Jensen developed a chamber that housed the radioisotope Cobalt-60. The remainder of this chamber is still located on the property of Oatland Island. After reading about experiments that the USDA conducted on the Screw Worm Fly, scientists at the Technical Development Laboratory wanted to try something similar with mosquitoes. A small pellet of the Cobalt-60 isotope was lowered six feet into the ground. When raised by a hydraulic device, the pellet exposed the mosquitoes to radiation. This technique was used to sterilize mosquitoes so that, after mating, the resulting eggs would not hatch. Dr. Richard Fay invented a device used to separate male pupae from the female pupae. Once the sterile male mosquitoes were released, there was a reduction in the mosquito population.

The Disinsection Project

After World War II, international air travel gained popularity, and the inadvertent transport of insect-borne diseases became an issue. Previously the flight crew would spray the cabin with aerosols on arrival. The smell was unpleasant and the results were ineffective. The WHO with the support of the Public Health Service initiated research to be done at the Technical Development Laboratory on Oatland Island. Under the direction of Dr. Pearce, Dr. Arnold Mattson began testing insecticides to determine what pesticides would kill insects at high altitudes. After testing numerous pesticides, Mattson found that Dipterex seemed to work. However, after several experiments, the pesticide failed to kill any of the insects. It was determined there was an impurity in the Dipterex. The Chemistry Section of the laboratory

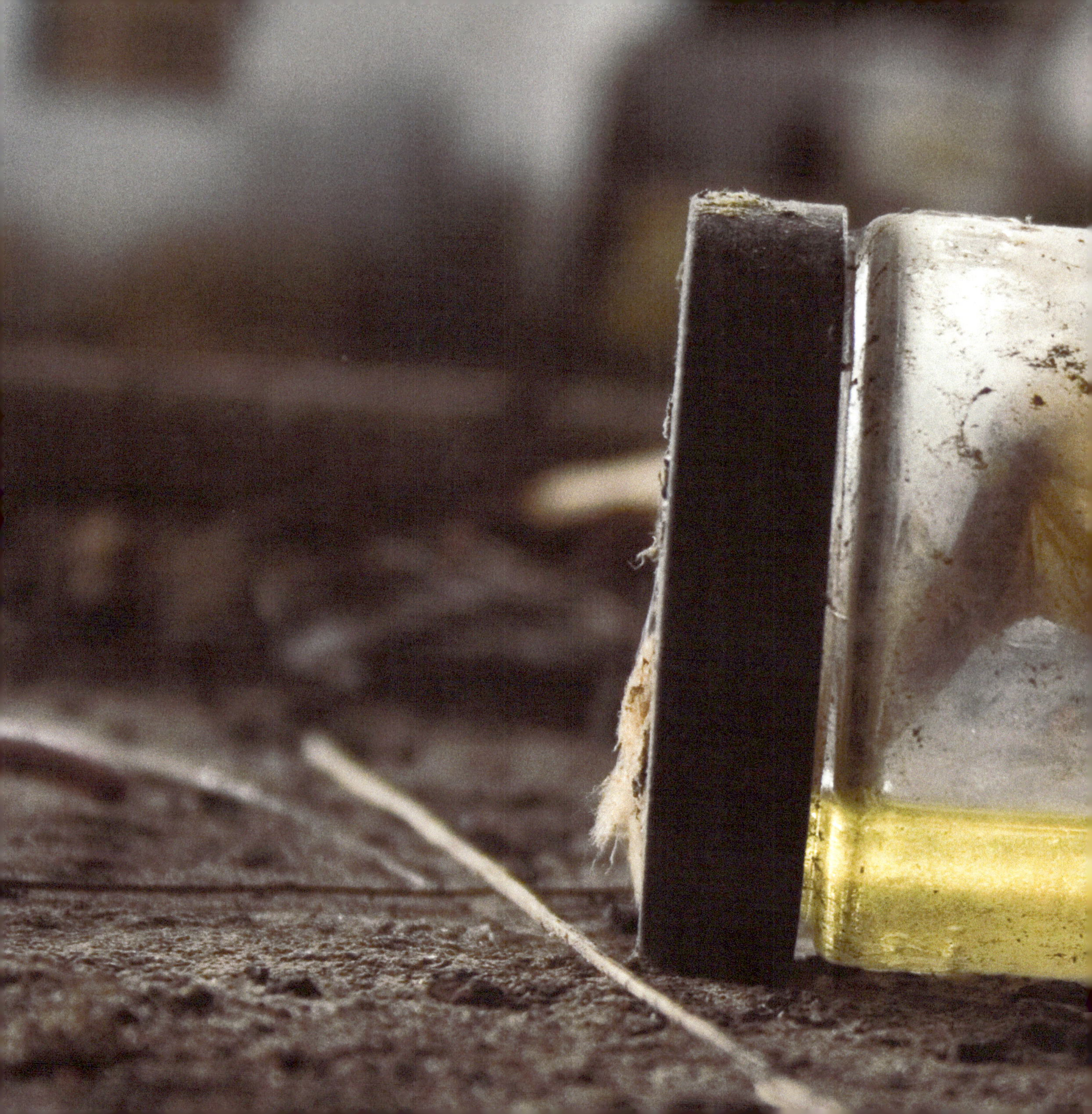

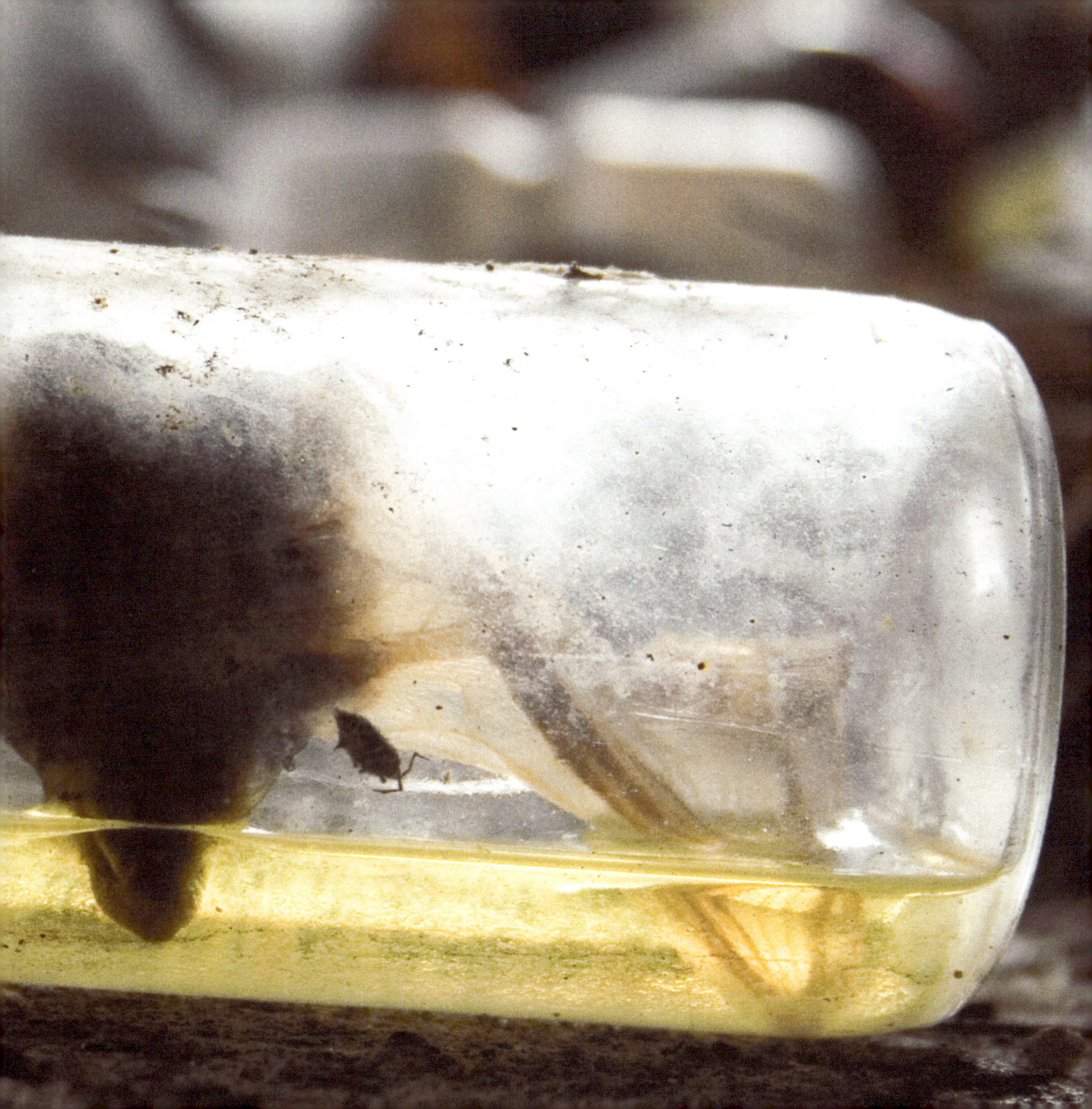

began studies to determine the impurity, and in the process they discovered a new compound, which was named DDVP or dicholovos.

Before DDVP could be approved for use in aircraft, many experiments had to be conducted to determine the way to deliver the DDVP through the planes. Mr. Jensen had the task of developing a DDVP system to be installed in passenger planes. He created a cartridge containing the compound that could be activated by a switch. A steam of air was sent through the cartridge which vaporized the DDVP, allowing it to be released through a steel tube that ran the length of the plane's ceiling. The system was installed in DC–6 and DC–7 aircrafts for testing. Dr. James Miles and several entomologists flew in these aircraft to conduct tests and find results from exposing the aircraft to DDVP. Dr. Miles reported that the tests were successful.

The research on DDVP did not end there. The scientists needed to determine if inhalation of the compound was safe for humans. Dr. W.J. Hayes contacted the Bureau of Prisons and received 60 volunteers from the Federal Prison Camp in Greenville, South Carolina. The prisoners were exposed to various levels of DDVP while they slept. Each morning they would undergo medical exams that tested their neurological statue, visual accuracy, and reaction time. The test results determined that the vapors were considered safe for the disinsection of the aircraft.

The Sausage Factory

A search began to determine other ways to use DDVP. Mr. Willis Mathis mixed 10% DDVP with Perlite, an amorphous volcanic glass, in a cup. The cup was then placed into a plastic bag and put in a room with mosquitoes. A few hours later the vapors had passed through the bag and killed the mosquitoes. The scientists determined that this would be valuable for household use; however, the formula proved to be unstable. Dr. James Miles began testing mixtures of DDVP with beeswax so that the vaporizers could be in solid form. His experiments led him to determine that mixing DDVP with montan wax and dibutyl phthalalte was effective. The production of solid vaporizers on Oatland Island then began.

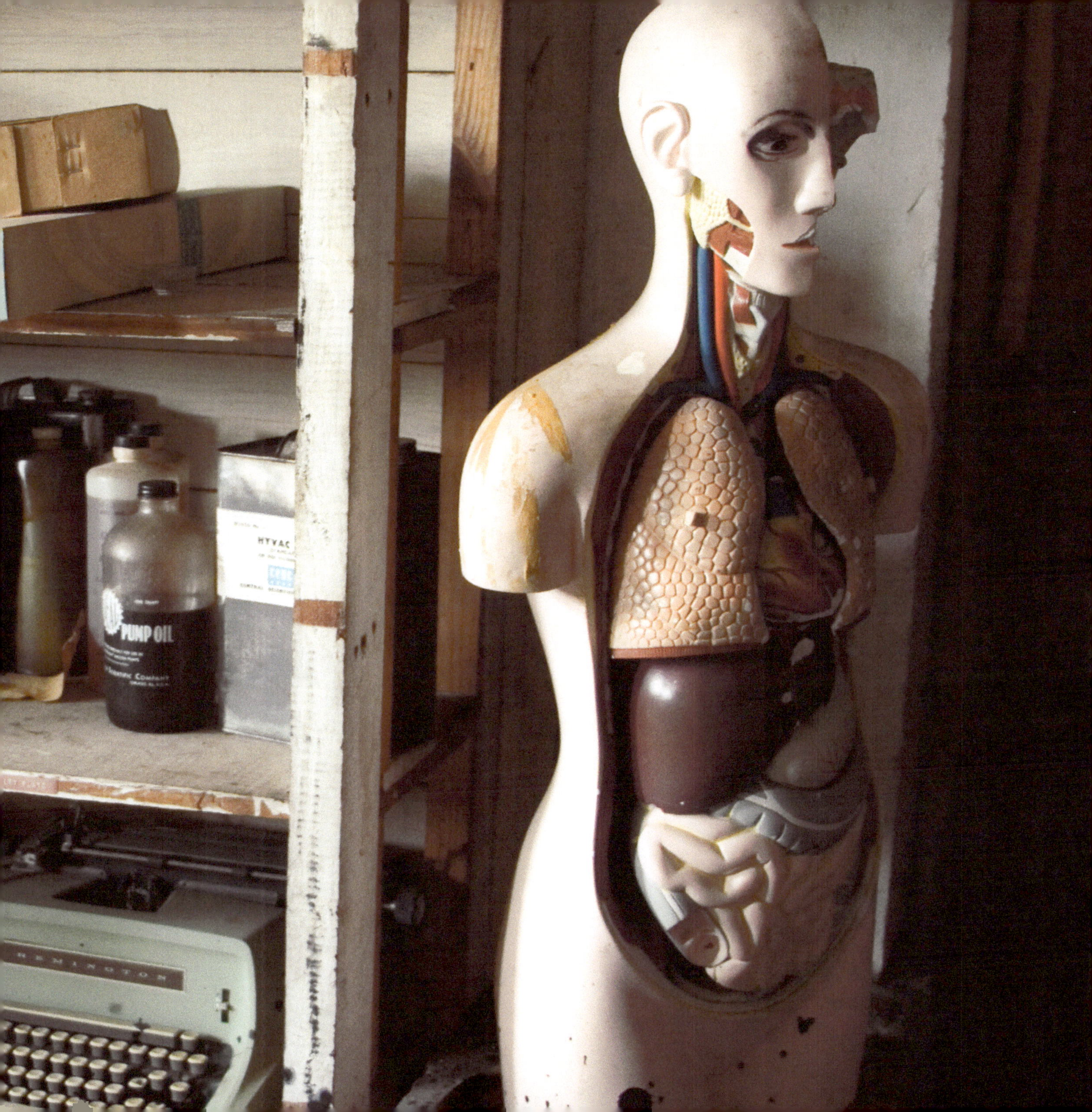
PUMP OIL
HYVAC
REMINGTON

n quantity on hand is
will not be restocked)

1-139-006	[illegible]
1-139-005	[illegible]
1-160-000	[illegible]
6505-153-8225	Ether, U.S.P., for anesthesia (1/2 lb. can)
51-L-50-100	Ether "Baker analyzed" reagent, AC, (5 lb. bottle)

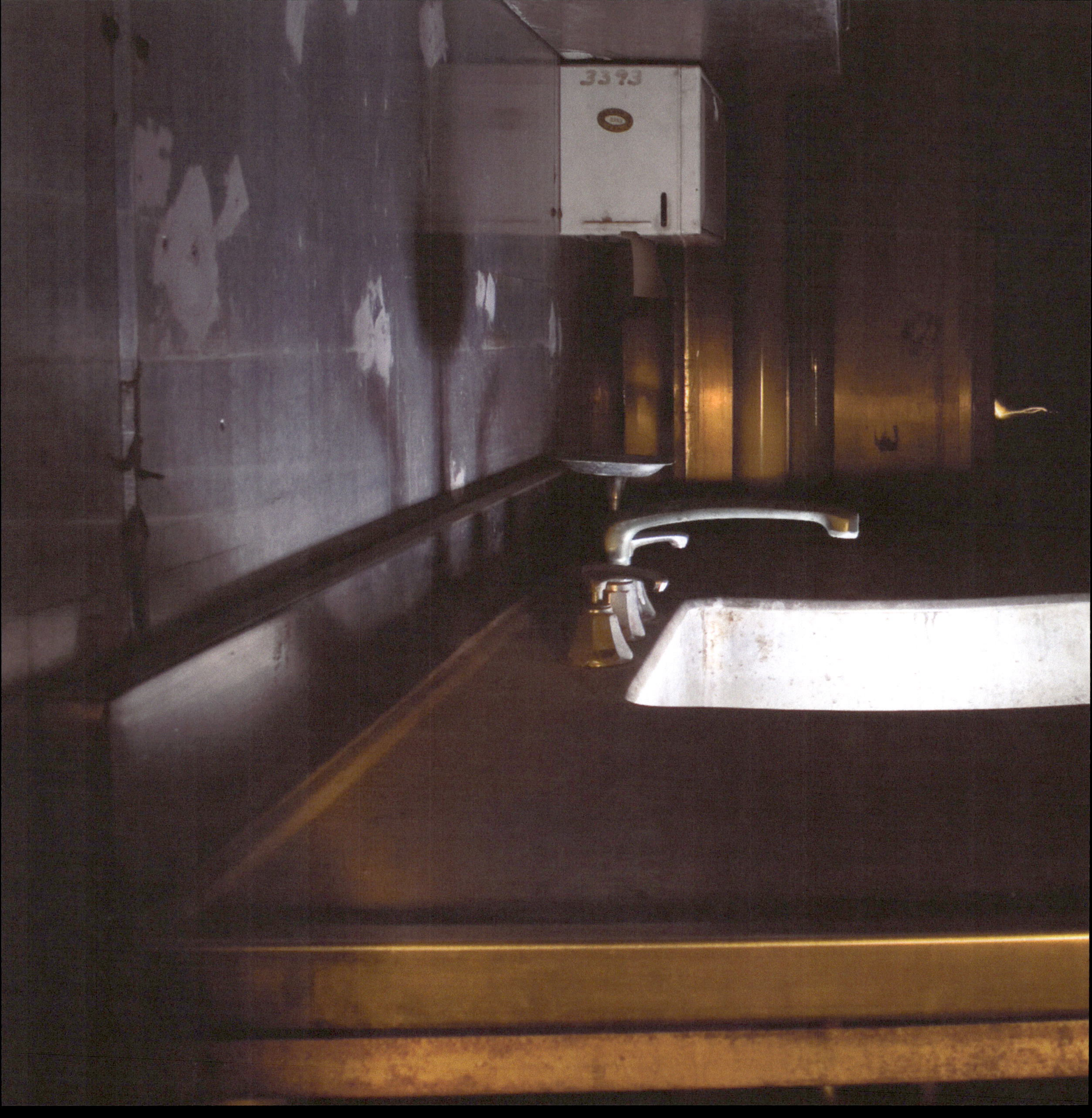
3393

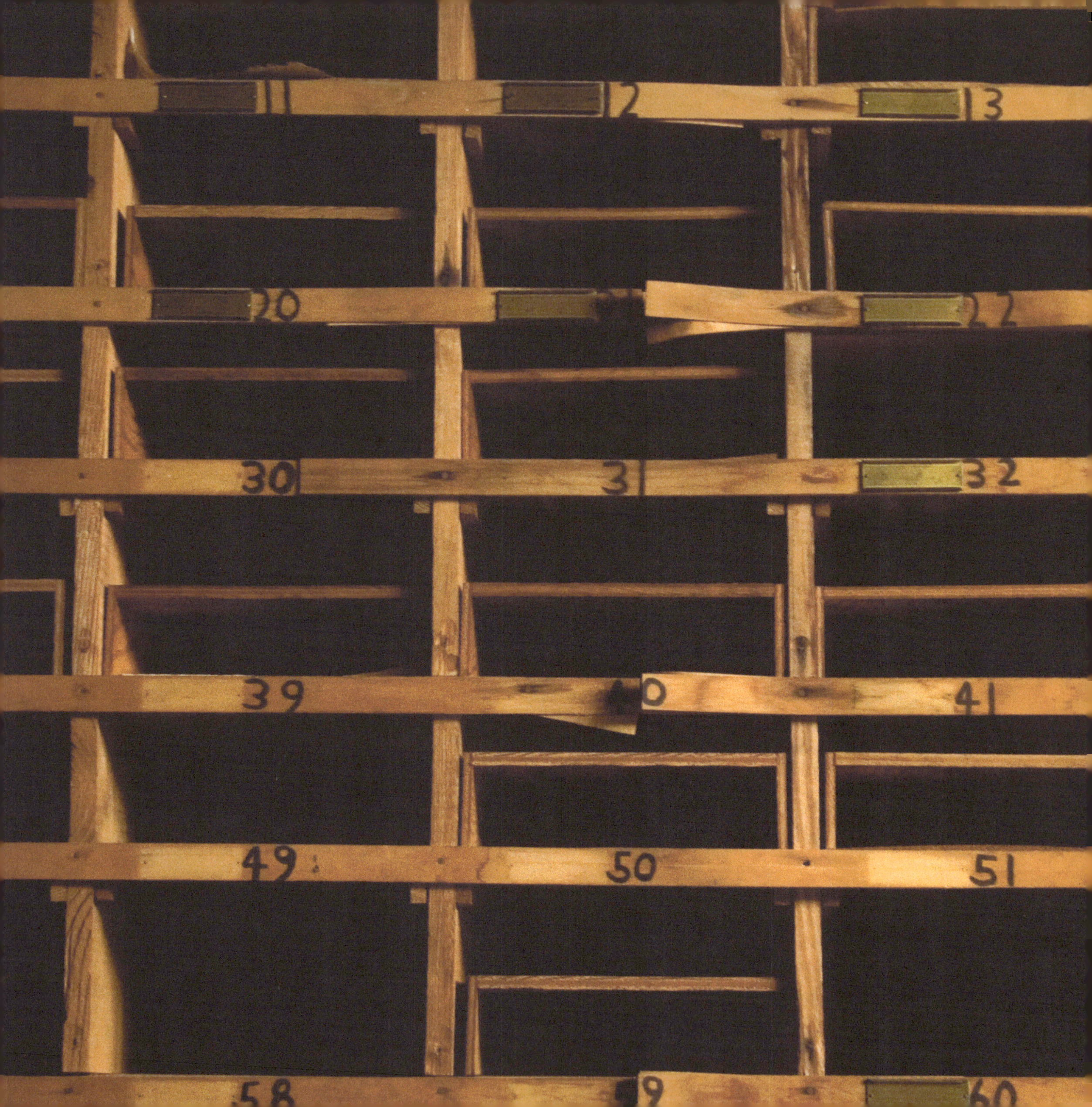
11
13
22
30
31
32
39
41
49
50
51
58
60

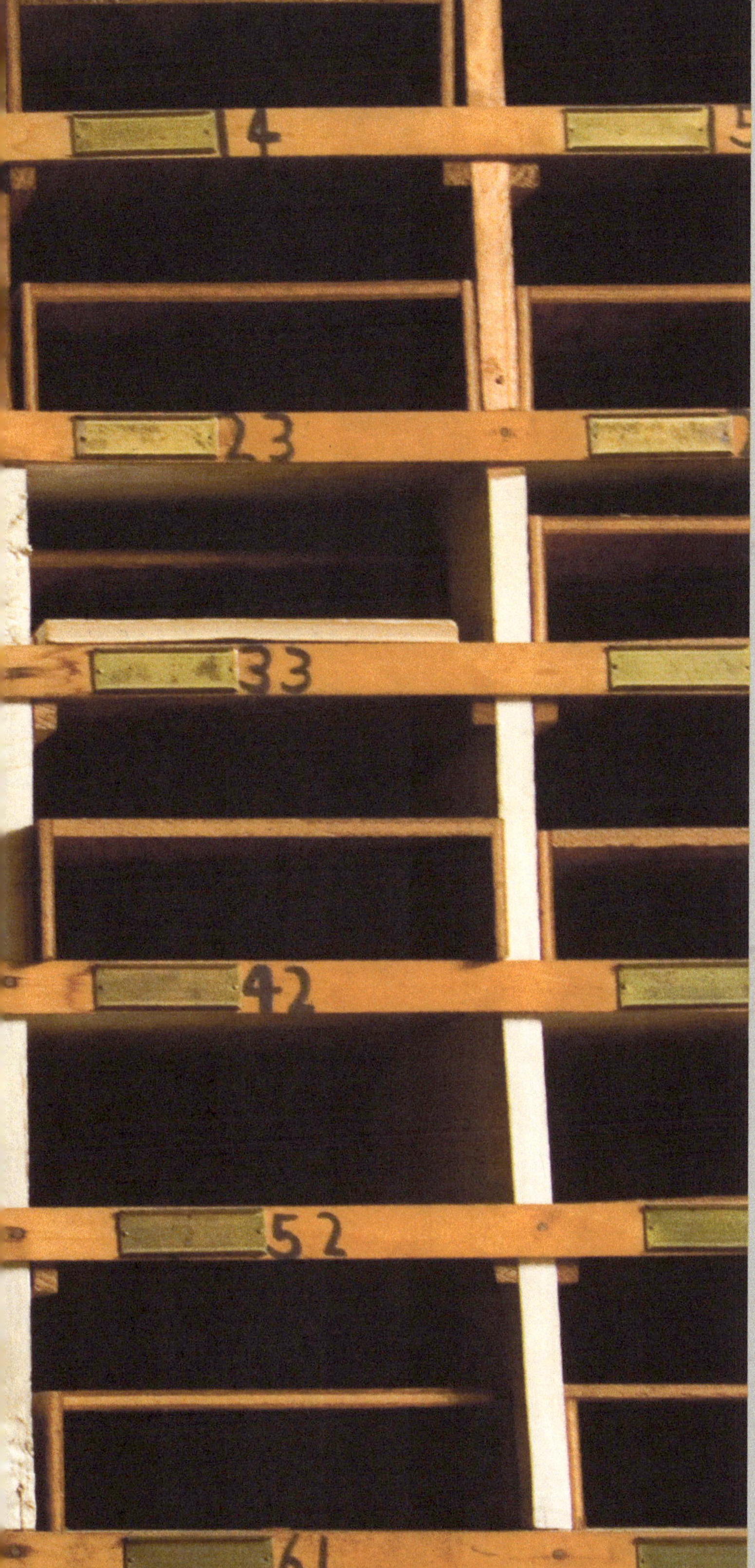

One of the metal buildings on Oatland Island was converted into a factory that produced the solid vaporizers. The ingredients were mixed inside a 30-gallon steel tank, equipped with a stirring device, a heating coil, and a tap on the bottom. After they were mixed and heated, a solution was discharged into 6-inch long plastic tubes. After the tubes cooled, they were cut apart and stored for shipping. Because the vaporizers looked like black sausages, the building was nicknamed the Sausage Factory.

Later, a more practical formula was found by mixing DDVP and polyvinyl chloride plastic (PVC). This formula, manufactured by the Shell Chemical Company, gained widespread household use under the name "No Pest Strips." In addition to controlling mosquitoes, it also was effective in controlling moths and flies.

The Toxicology Section

The Toxicology Section, led by Dr. Hayes, conducted many controversial experiments on the effect of pesticides on humans. Dr. Arnold Mattson studied DDT in human fat. Because DDT was so widespread, most humans had traces of it in their fat. To find individuals that were DDT free, Mattson used samples from cadavers that passed away before the pesticide was used. Twenty–four volunteers from the Federal Bureau of Prisons ingested a small amount of DDT per day over a period of 18 months. Daily medical exams found that none of the prisoners were affected.

In the 1960s, the CDC began hearing reports of disoriented crop–duster pilots crashing their planes. The pilots were spraying their crops with a pesticide called parathion. The Toxicology Section set out to determine if the pilots were becoming ill from inhalation of parathion or from skin absorption. Because Dr. Pearce was absolutely certain that the cause was from inhalation, he and Dr. Steve Miller allowed the substance to be poured on their backs. Blood samples, urine samples, and tests for cholinesterase depression were taken at thirty–minute intervals. The results were negative, and immediately the crop dusters were supplied with oxygen masks. The problem was solved. Dr. James Miles states that this experiment was never published.

1973

TDL Moves to Atlanta, GA

The Technical Development Laboratory's research continued on Oatland Island until 1973. The laboratory was moved to Atlanta, Georgia to the headquarters of the CDC.

1974

Oatland Island Education Center

In 1974, The Savannah Board of Education acquired Oatland Island and established Oatland Island Education Center as a unit of Savannah–Chatham County Public School system. Through a variety of educational programs, the staff members promote environmental awareness to the community, students, and teachers. In addition to the educational programs, Oatland Island is home to a variety of animals.

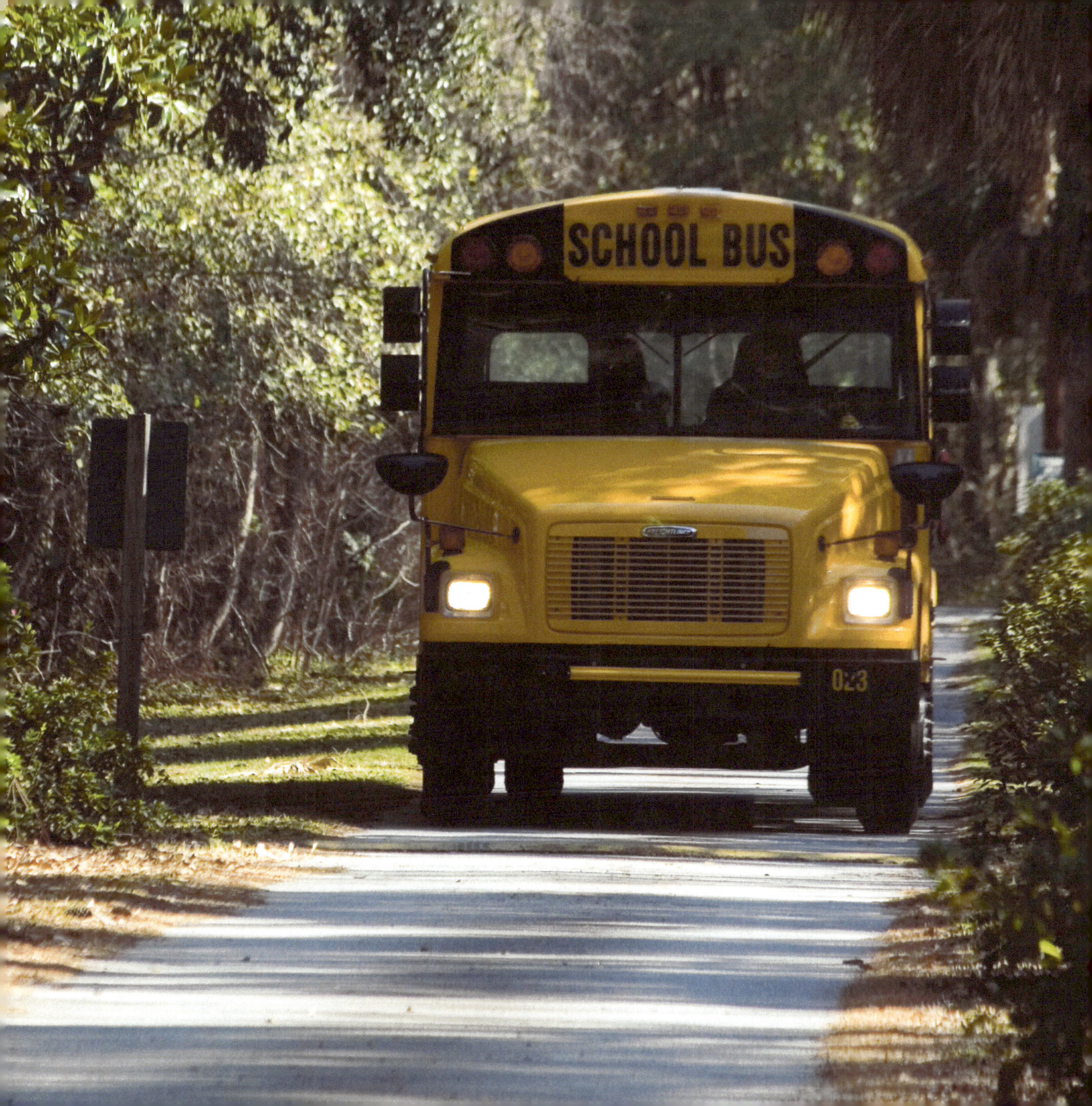
SCHOOL BUS
023

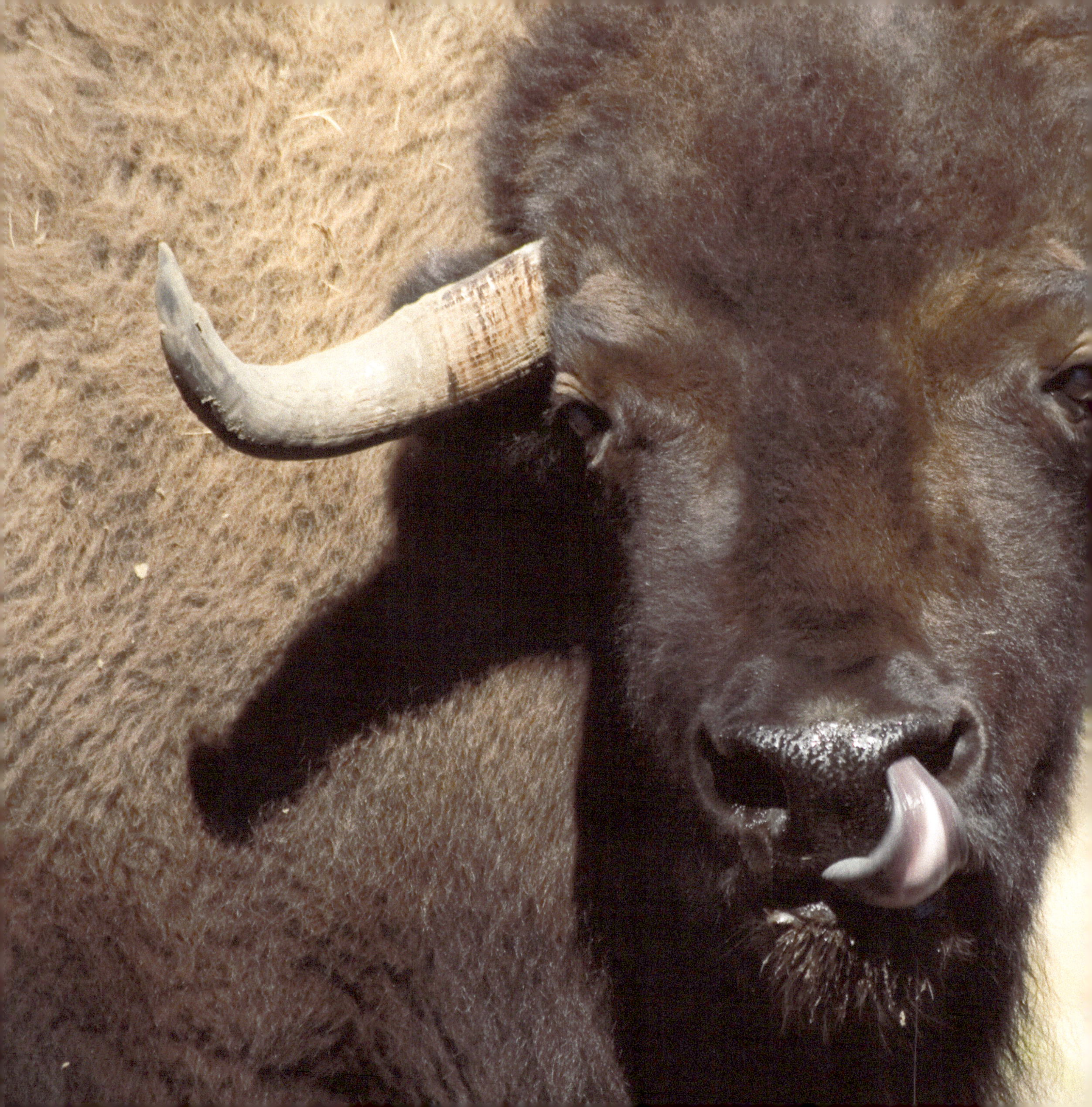

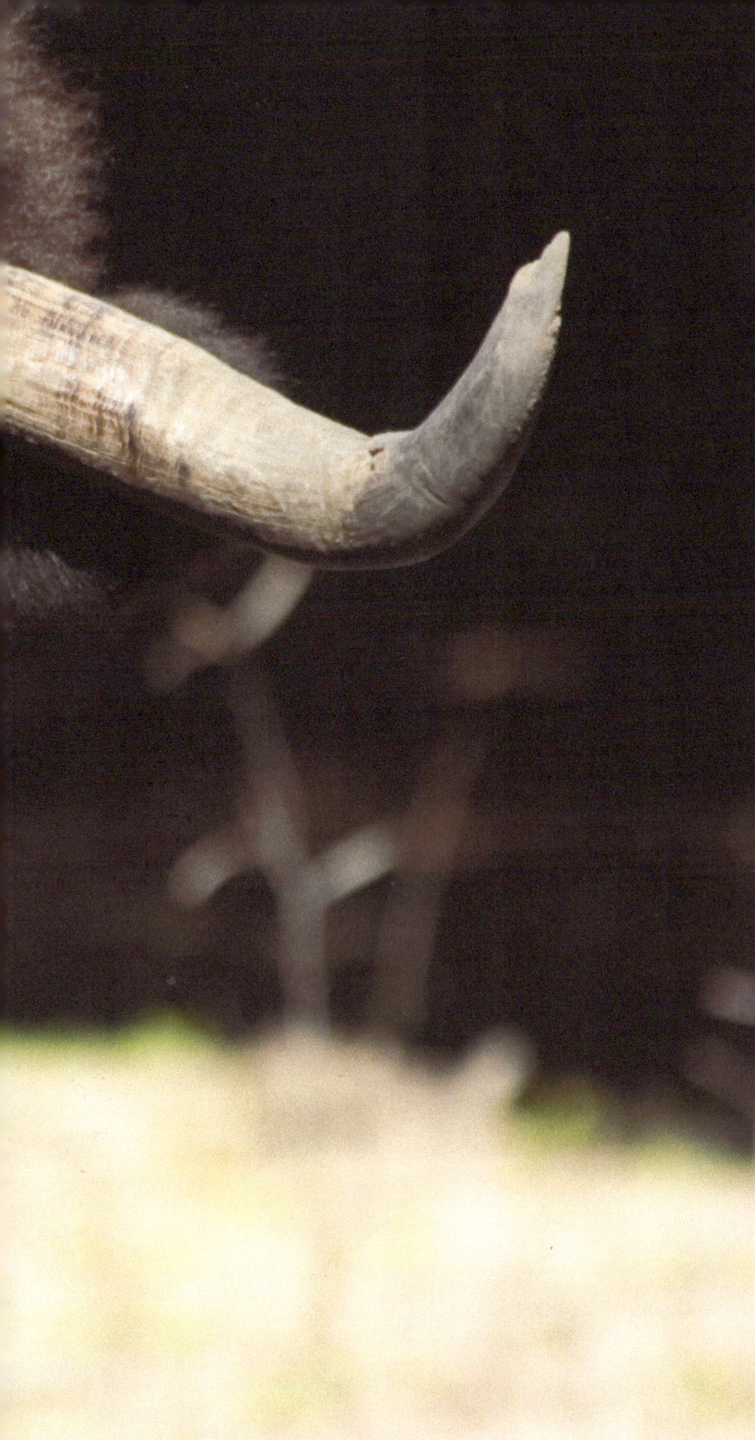

While walking along the nature trails, visitors can observe pelicans, wolves, fox, bobcats, Florida panthers, many species of birds, and more.

2007

Oatland Island Wildlife Center

In 2007, Oatland Island Education Center was renamed Oatland Island Wildlife Center of Savannah. Today the center is recognized as the premier environmental education center in the southeastern United States.

Oatland Island is open to the public Monday through Friday from 9:00 AM to 4:00 PM and most Saturdays from 10:00 AM to 4:00 PM. Throughout the year, Oatland hosts a variety of events including the Medieval Festival, The Halloween Hike, The Cane Grinding and Harvest Festival, and the Sheep to Shawl Festival.

Oatland Island Wildlife Center relies on gifts, donations, and grants to help maintain the facilities and feed the animals. For information on how to donate, visit the Oatland Island web site at http://www.oatlandisland.org or call 912-898-3980.

List of Resources

"DDT Ban Takes Effect." U.S. Environmental Protection Agency: EPA press release. 31 Dec. 1972. <http://www.epa.gov/history/topics/ddt/01.htm>.

Emsley, John. Molecules at an Exhibition: Portraits of Intriguing Materials in Everyday Life.Oxford University Press: Oxford, 1998.

Genrich, Pam. "Betty's Story." Oatland Island Education Center. 22 Sept. 2003.

Gratz, Norman G., Robert Steffen, and William Cocksedge."Why aircraft disinsection?" Bulletin of the World Health Organization. 2000.

Jensen, Jens A. , and Richard W. Fay. "Tagging of Adult House Flies and Flesh Flies with Radioactive Phosphorus." The American Society of Tropical Medicine and Hygiene.1951. <http://www.ajtmh.org/cgi/content/abstract/s1-31/4/523>.

MacLeod, Marcie. "Oatland Island's Technical Development Laboratories—Active In the Fight Against Disease For 25 Years." Savannah Morning News. 27 April 1969.

Miles, Dr. James. "The History of Oatland Circa 1790-1973: With recollections from Dr. James Miles, Chemist with the Centers for Disease Control." February, 2006.

"Montan wax." Wikipedia, The Free Encyclopedia. 26 Apr 2007, 21:19 UTC. Wikimedia Foundation, Inc. <http://en.wikipedia.org/w/index.php?title=Montan_wax&oldid=126238390>.

Parascandola, John. "From MCWA to CDC—Origins of the Centers for Disease Control and Prevention." Public Health Papers. November/December 1996. Volume 111.

Pearce, Mallory. "Preserving Oatland: Oatland's 30 Year Past." Connect Savannah. <http://www.connectsavannah.com/show_article.php?article_id=1161315655>.

"Perlite." Wikipedia, The Free Encyclopedia. 22 Mar 2007, 12:29 UTC. Wikimedia Foundation, Inc. <http://en.wikipedia.org/w/index.php?title=Perlite&oldid=117013416>.

"Radioisotope." MedicineNet.com. MedicineNet, Inc., 1996–2007.<http://www.medterms.com/script/main/art.asp?articlekey=5188>.

Stephens, Nelson, T. "International Conductors DedicateTheir New Home Here Tomorrow." Savannah Morning News. 9 Nov. 1927.

"The History of the CDC." National Center for Infectious Diseases, Division of Parasitic Diseases. 23, April 2004. <http://www.cdc.gov/about/history.htm>.

"The History of Malaria, an Ancient Disease." National Center for Infectious Diseases, Division of Parasitic Diseases. 23, April 2004. <http://www.cdc.gov/malaria/history/index.htm#eradicationworldwide>.

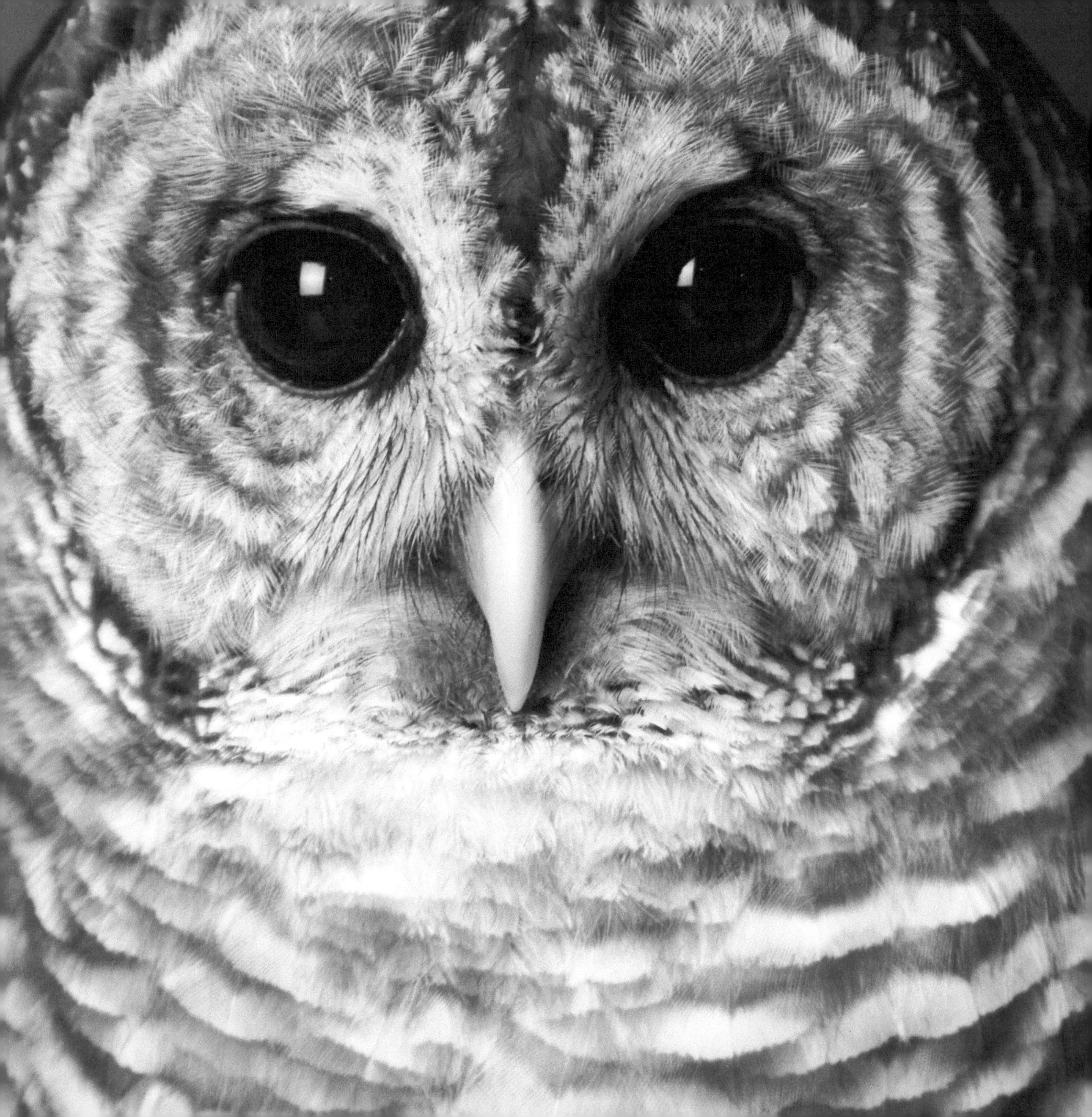

About the Author

Tara Parekh was born in Towson, Maryland in 1981 and grew up in Churchville, Maryland. She graduated from the Rochester Institute of Technology in 2003 with a Bachelor of Science degree in New Media Publishing, and furthered her education with a Master of Arts degree in Digital Photography from the Savannah College of Art and Design. You may contact her via email at tarpar@gmail.com.